Granville Sharp

The Law of Passive Obedience

Or Christian submission to personal injuries

Granville Sharp

The Law of Passive Obedience
Or Christian submission to personal injuries

ISBN/EAN: 9783337411367

Printed in Europe, USA, Canada, Australia, Japan

Cover: Foto ©Lupo / pixelio.de

More available books at **www.hansebooks.com**

THE LAW

OF

PASSIVE OBEDIENCE,

OR

Chriſtian Submiſſion to Perſonal Injuries:

Wherein is ſhewn, that the ſeveral texts of ſcripture, which command the entire ſubmiſſion of *ſervants* or *ſlaves* to their *maſters*, cannot authorize the latter *to exact an involuntary ſervitude*, nor, in the leaſt degree, juſtify the claims of modern *Slaveholders*.

By GRANVILLE SHARP.

' SERVANTS, *obey in all things* (your) *maſters, accord-*
' *ing to the fleſh; not with eye ſervice, as men pleaſers, but*
' *in ſingleneſs of heart, fearing God:*' &c. Coloſſ. iii. 22.

THE
LAW of PASSIVE OBEDIENCE,
OR
CHRISTIAN SUBMISSION to PERSONAL INJURIES.

THE illegality of slavery among Christians is a point which I have long laboured to demonstrate, as being destructive of morality, and consequently dangerous both to body and soul. There are nevertheless some particular Texts in the New Testament, which, in the opinion even of several well meaning and disinterested persons, seem to afford some proof of the toleration of slavery among the primitive Christians; and, from thence, they are induced

induced to conceive, *that Christianity doth not oblige its professors to renounce the practice of slaveholding.*

A learned and reverend correspondent of mine seems to have adopted this notion, and has signified his opinion nearly to the same effect, in a private letter to me on this subject, to which I have not yet ventured to send him a reply, though it is a considerable time since I received his letter; but, to say the truth, the question in which I had never before apprehended any difficulty, was rendered very serious and important, upon my hands, by my friend's declaration; and I thought myself bound to give it the strictest examination, because I conceived (as I do still) that the honour of the Holy Scriptures, which of all other things, I have most at heart, was concerned in the determination of the point in question; and yet I know, that my friend

friend is full as zealous for the honour of the Scriptures as myself, and much more learned in them, being very eminent in that most essential branch of knowledge.

I believe also that he is perfectly disinterested, and of undoubted *Christian benevolence*. The objection has therefore acquired an accumulated weight from the authority and worth of the person who made it; and consequently, it demanded more circumspection and reading, to answer it in any reasonable time, than my short broken intervals of leisure (the only time that I was then master of) would permit me to bestow upon it; and as so much time has already elapsed, the answer which I originally intended for my friend's private perusal, shall now be addressed to all well meaning persons in general, who may have had the same motives for admitting in any degree the

legality

legality of slavery; and that there are many such (even among those that are concerned in the practice of slaveholding) the example of my disinterested friend's opinion, and common charity, oblige me to suppose. I shall therefore consider my friend's opinion as the common excuse of our American and West Indian brethren for tolerating slavery a-among them.

'*I do not think* (says he) *that Chris-*
'*tianity released slaves from the obligation*
'*they were under according to the custom*
'*and law of the Countries, where it was*
'*propagated.*'

This objection to my general doctrine *is* expressed in the most *guarded* terms; —so *guarded*, that it obliges me to acknowledge, that the observation is, in some respects, strictly *true*. My present attempt is not to confute, but rather

rather to demonstrate wherein this *truth* consists, which will afterwards enable me to point out such a due limitation of the doctrine, as will render it entirely consistent with the hypothesis, which I have so long laboured to maintain, viz. *the absolute illegality of slavery among Christians,*

In conformity to my worthy friend's declaration I must first observe, that the disciples of Christ (whose *Kingdom,* he himself declared,—' *is not of* THIS ' WORLD.' John xviii. 36.) had no *express* commission to alter *the* TEMPORAL CONDITION OF MEN, but only to prepare them for a BETTER WORLD by the general doctrines of *faith, hope, charity, peace and goodwill,* (or universal love and benevolence to all mankind) *submission to injuries, dependence upon God,* &c. &c. &c. which (though *general* doctrines) are amply and sufficiently

ciently efficacious indeed, for the *particular* reformation of ALL CONDITIONS OF MEN, when *sincerity* is not wanting in the application of them; but the principal intention of the whole system is evidently to draw men from the the cares and anxieties of *this present life,* to a better hope in the *life to come,* which is Christ's proper kingdom: Christian servants therefore were of course instructed to be *patient,* to be *humble* and *submissive* to their masters, 'not only to the good and gentle, but also to the *froward.*' So that even *ill usage* does not justify *perverseness* of behaviour in christian slaves.

THE apostle *Paul* also frequently insists upon the absolute necessity of an unfeigned obedience in the behaviour of christian servants to their masters. 'Let every man abide in the same calling wherein he was called.' 'Art thou called

' *called being a servant? care not for it;*"
&c. 1 Cor. vii. 21. and again, ' *Ser-*
' *vants be obedient to them that are (your)*
' *masters according to the flesh, with fear*
' *and trembling, in singleness of your*
' *heart as unto Christ; not with eye service,*
' *as men pleasers, but as the servants of*
' *Christ, doing the Will of God from the*
' *heart; with good will doing service, as to*
' *the Lord, and not to men: knowing that*
' *whatsoever good thing any man doeth, the*
' *same shall he receive of the Lord, whe-*
' *ther he be bond or free,*" Ephef. vi 5-8.
' Again, ' *Servants obey in all things*
' *(your) masters according to the flesh; not*
' *with eye service, as men pleasers, but*
' *in singleness of heart fearing God: and*
' *whatever you do, do it heartily, as to*
' *the Lord, and not unto men.*' Colof. iii.
' 22, 23. The same apostle instructs *Ti-*
' *mothy* to recommend obedience to ser-
' vants, ' *Let as many servants* (says the
' apostle) *as are under the yoke, count*

B   ' *their*

' *their own masters worthy of all honour,*
' *that* THE NAME OF GOD AND HIS
' DOCTRINE BE NOT BLASPHEMED.
' *And they that have believing masters, let*
' *them not despise* (them) BECAUSE THEY
' ARE BRETHREN; BUT RATHER DO
' (them) SERVICE, BECAUSE THEY
' ARE FAITHFUL AND BELOVED PAR-
' TAKERS OF THE BENEFIT. *These*
' *things teach and exhort: If any man*
' *teach otherwise, and consent not to whole-*
' *some words,* (even) *the words of our*
' *Lord Jesus Christ, and to the doctrine*
' *which is according to godliness; he is*
' *proud, knowing nothing, but doting*
' *about questions, and strifes of words,*
' *whereof cometh envy, strife, railings,*
' *evil-surmisings, perverse disputings of*
' *men of corrupt minds, and destitute of*
' *the truth, supposing that gain is godli-*
' *ness. From such withdraw thyself. But*
' *godliness with contentment is great gain.*
' *for we brought nothing into* (this) *world,*
' *and*

'*and it is certain we can carry nothing
'*out. And having food and raiment, let
'*us be therewith content.*' 1 Tim. vi.
'*1 to 8.*—And again he infists on the
'*same doctrine, '* (Exhort) *servants,*
'*(says he) to be obedient unto their own
'*masters, (and) to please (them) well in all
'*things, not answering again, not pur-
'*loining, but shewing all good fidelity;
'*that they may* ADORN THE DOC-
'TRINE OF GOD OUR SAVIOUR IN
'ALL THINGS.' Titus ii. 9, 10.

THESE Texts are amply sufficient to prove the truth of my learned friend's assertion, so far as it relates to THE DUTY OF THE SLAVES THEMSELVES, but this *absolute submission* required of Christian servants, by no means implies the *legality* of slaveholding ON THE PART OF THEIR MASTERS, which *he* seems to apprehend.

THE slave violates no precepts of the gospel by his abject condition, provided that the same is *involuntary* (for if he can be made free, he is expresly commanded by the apostle to *use it rather* §) but how the master who enforces *that involuntary servitude*, can be said to act consistently with the Christian profession, is a question of a very different nature, which I propose to examine with all possible care and impartiality, being no otherwise interested in it, than as a Christian who esteems both masters and slaves as brethren, and consequently, while he pities the unhappy *temporal condition* of the latter, is extremely anxious for the *eternal welfare* of the former.

I

---

§ *Art thou called* (being) *a servant? care not for it;* BUT IF THOU MAYEST BE MADE FREE, USE IT RATHER. *For he that is called in the lord* (being) *a servant, is the lord's freeman, &c.* ' *ye are bought with a price,* 'BE NOT YE THE SERVANTS OF MEN.' 1 Cor. vii. 21-23.

I HAVE already admitted, that CHRISTIANITY DOTH NOT RELEASE SLAVES, 'from the obligation they were under according to the custom and law of the countries where it was propagated,' agreeable to my learned friend's assertion, in favour of which I have produced a variety of texts: but as '*the reason of the law*,' (according to a maxim of the *English* law) '*is the life of the law,*' we cannot with justice draw any conclusion from thence, in favour of the master's claim, till we have examined the principles, on which the doctrine *of submission*, in these several texts, is founded; and we shall find, upon a general view of the whole, that the principal reason of enforcing the doctrine was not so much because the persons to whom it was addressed, *were slaves*, as because they *were Christians*, and were to overcome EVIL

with

with GOOD, to the GLORY OF GOD *and* RELIGION.

THESE principles are clearly *expressed* in several of these very texts, and *implied* in all of them, viz. 'That the name of God and his doctrine be not blasphemed.' (1 Tim. vi. 1.) and again, 'that they 'may adorn the doctrine of God our Savi- 'our IN ALL THINGS.' (Titus ii. 10.) So that a zeal for the GLORY OF GOD, and of HIS RELIGION (the principles of the first great commandment) is the apparent ground and sole purpose of the Christian *slave's* SUBMISSION, which was therefore to be ' WITH SINGLE-
' NESS OF HEART AS UNTO CHRIST.'
' *not with eye service*, AS MEN PLEASERS,
' *but as* THE SERVANTS OF CHRIST,
' *doing the will of God from the heart;*
' *with good will doing service*, AS TO THE
' LORD, *and* NOT TO MEN : *knowing*
' *that whatsoever good thing any man doeth,*
' *the same shall* HE RECEIVE OF THE
LORD,

'Lord, *whether he* BE BOND OR FREE.' Ephef. vi. 5-8. And again, the fame apoftle charges the fervants among the Coloffians, to obey ' *not* AS MEN PLEA-' SERS, *but in finglenefs of heart,* FEAR-' ING GOD : *and whatfoever they do, to* ' *do it heartil* , *as* TO THE LORD, *and* ' NOT UNTO MEN.' Coloff. iii. 2.

THUS it is plain that the fervice was to be performed ' AS TO THE LORD,' and ' NOT TO MEN,' and therefore it cannot be conftrued as an acknowledgement of any *right,* or *property* really vefted *in the mafter.* This will clearly appear upon a clofer examination of fome of thefe texts. In the firft, for inftance, though the apoftle *Peter* enforces the neceffity of the fervants *fubmiffion* to their mafters, in the ftrongeft manner, commanding them to be fubject ' *not only to* ' *the good and gentle, but* ALSO TO THE FROWARD,' &c. (1. Pet. ii. 18.)
yet

yet he adds in the very next verse,—— '*for this is thank worthy, if a man,* FOR CONSCIENCE TOWARDS GOD, *endure grief,* SUFFERING *wrongfully*,'—πασχων αδικως,' so that, it is manifest, the apostle did not mean to *justify* the claim of the masters, because he enjoined the same submission to the servants that suffered *wrongfully,* as to those who had good and gentle masters: and it would be highly injurious to the *gospel of peace,* to suppose it capable of authorizing *wrongful sufferings,* or of establishing a *right* or power in any rank of men whatever, to oppress others *unjustly,* or αδικως! And though the apostle *Paul,* also, so strongly exhorts servants to submit to their masters, and '*to abide in the same calling wherein they were called,*' and '*not to care for it.*' (1 Corinthians, vii. 20, 21.) Yet at the same time he clearly instructs them, that it is their duty to prefer a state of *freedom* whenever they can fairly and honestly

obtain

obtain it; '*but if thou mayeſt be made* '*free* (ſays he) USE IT RATHER.' (V.21.) And the reaſon, which he aſſigns for this command, is as plainly delivered, viz. *the equality of ſervants with their maſters in the ſight of the Almighty,* '*For he* '*that is called in the Lord,* (being) *a* SER-
'VANT (ſays he) *is the Lord's* FREE-
'MAN: LIKEWISE, *alſo he that is call-*
'*ed* (being) FREE, *is Chriſt's* SERVANT.' (verſe 22.) *Chriſt* having purchaſed all men to be his *peculiar ſervants,* or rather *freemen.* '*Ye are bought with a* '*price* ſays the apoſtle, in the 23d verſe.) 'BE NOT YE THE SERVANTS OF MEN,' which plainly implies, that it is inconſiſtent with the dignity of a Chriſtian, who is the *ſervant* or *freeman of* GOD, to be held in an *unlimited* ſubjection, as the bond *ſervant* or *ſlave of a* MAN; and, conſequently, that a toleration of ſlavery, in places where Chriſtianity is eſtabliſhed by law, is intirely illegal;

for tho' THE SLAVE commits no crime by submitting to the *involuntary service,* (which has been already demonstrated,) yet the CHRISTIAN MASTER is guilty of a sort of sacriledge, by appropriating to himself, as an *absolute property,* that body, which *peculiarly belongs to God by an inestimable purchase!* For if God said of the Jews, even under the old law, (Levit. xxv. 52.) ' THEY ' ARE MY SERVANTS, *which I* ' *brought forth out of the land of Egypt;* " THEY SHALL NOT BE SOLD " AS BONDMEN.' ‡ How much more

‡ My learned friend, (mentioned in the beginning of this Tract) has remarked that ' *tho' God expressed* ' *himself concerning the Jews under the law in this* ' *manner.* " THEY ARE MY SERVANTS, WHICH I " BROUGHT FORTH OUT OF THE LAND OF EGYPT, " THEY SHALL NOT BE SOLD AS BONDMEN " &c. yet ' *This did not signify* (says he*) that they were not to be* ' *slaves at all. They might be slaves for seven years, as is* ' *well known, notwithstanding they were God's redeemed ser-* ' *vants. Nay, they might remain slaves 'till the jubilee,*
' WITH

more ought Christians to esteem their *brethren,* as *the peculiar servants of* GOD on account of their being *freed* from the more *severe bondage* of our spiritual ene-

my,

'WITH THEIR OWN CONSENT, *at the expiration of that*
'*short term of involuntary servitude.* These *words indeed*
'*contained a declaration that none of the Israelites were*
'*to be slaves for ever like the Heathen.* But *what a slip-*
'*pery proof,* (says he) *of this exemption with regard to*
'*Christians?* How *dangerous* (continued he,) *is it to*
'*build doctrines upon such parallels and comparisons!*' But my worthy friend seems to forget that the kind of slavery which I oppose, is not that *limited temporary servitude,* which he describes *as consistent with the law,* for that differs very little from the condition of *hired servants,* in which light, the Hebrew masters were *bound by the law,* to look upon their brethren, even though bought with their money as bond servants or slaves,' *If*
'*thy brother* (that dwelleth) *by thee be waxen poor,* and
'BE SOLD *unto thee;* THOU SHATL NOT COMPEL HIM
'TO SERVE AS A BOND SERVANT: (but) AS AN HIRED
'SERVANT AND AS A SOJOURNER, *he shall be with thee,*
'and *shall serve thee unto the year of* Jubile. *And then*
'*shall he depart from thee,* (both) *he and his children with*
'*him,* &c. *For they are my servants,* (said the Almighty)
'THEY SHALL NOT BE SOLD AS BOND-MEN.'

' THOU

my, (of which the *Egyptian bondage* was only a type) by the ineſtimable price of Chriſt's blood! and, ſurely, we may therefore ſay, '*they* are GOD'S SER-'VANTS,' whom Chriſt hath redeemed with his own blood, as much as the Jews of old, who were on that account expreſly *enfranchiſed* from worldly bondage, 'THEY ARE MY SERVANTS, 'THEY SHALL NOT BE SOLD AS 'BONDMEN;' for this application of the text is entirely to the ſame effect as the apoſtle's expreſſion to the Corinthians,-------'*Ye are bought with* '*a price*, BE NOT YE THE SERVANTS OF MEN.' (1. Cor. vii. 23.)

Dr.

'THOU SHALT NOT RULE OVER HIM WITH RI-'GOUR, *but ſhalt fear thy God*.' Levit. xxv. 39, 43. Here is the very *text*, (with it's *context*) which I had quoted, to ſhew the *illegality* of holding a *brother* Iſraelite in abſolute ſlavery, and as I have elſewere fully demonſtrated that men of all nations are to be conſidered as *brethren* under the goſpel diſpenſation, ſo my learned friend ſurely does great injuſtice to the argument, when he calls it '*a ſlip-* '*pery*

Dr. *Whitby*, indeed suppoſes that the words '*ye are bought with a price*,' refer only to a pecuniary price given by the primitive Chriſtians, *to buy their brethren out of ſlavery*.' But the authority of *Juſtin Martyr* and *Tertullian*, which he cites, by no means proves his interpretation of the text, tho' it may ſufficiently prove the primitive practice of *redeeming ſlaves*; which alſo furniſhes a new argument againſt the legality of *ſlavery among Chriſtians*, ſo far

'*pery proof* of *this exemption with regard to Chriſ-*
'*tians*,' and aſſerts that the text in queſtion *does not ſignify that they* (the Iſraelites) *were not to be ſlaves at all!* It clearly *ſignifies* however, that whatſoever *right* a maſter might have acquired (even by an abſolute *purchaſe*) over his Hebrew brother, yet that he was ſtill required to treat him as an *hired ſervant*, and to diſcharge *him* and *his* at a *limited time:* and when we compare it with the parallel text in Deuteronomy, (xv. 12, 14.) we find the maſter is there ſtrictly enjoined to reward the Bond-man LIBERALLY for his paſt ſervices, viz. ' *And when thou ſendeſt him out free from thee*, THOU
' SHALT FURNISH HIM LIBERALLY *out of thy*
' *flock, and out of thy floor, and out of thy wine preſs*,' &c. Surely when the true nature of ſuch *limited ſervitude* is

far as the example of the *primitive Chriſtians* is concerned. But ſcripture is beſt interpreted by ſcripture, and therefore the moſt certain means of aſcertaining the true meaning of the words τιμης ηγορασθητε, ‘ *ye are bought with* ‘ *a price,*’ is to have recourſe to the very ſame expreſſion (ηγορασθητε γαρ τιμης, the words being only tranſpoſed) in the preceding chapter, 20th verſe, where we ſhall find that it can refer to nothing leſs than the ineſtimable price of Chriſt's redemption, ‘ *What know ye not* (ſays ‘ the apoſtle) *that your* BODY *is the* TEM-
‘ PLE

is duly conſidered, it affords but ‘ *a ſlippery* proof,’ (if I may uſe my friend's expreſſion) ‘ that *they were to* ‘ *be ſlaves at all,*’ at leaſt, ‘ *at all,*’ in the ſenſe contended for by our American and Weſt India ſlaveholders (which is the only matter in diſpute at preſent) eſpecially as the condition of a *hired ſervant* is expreſsly mentioned, as the rank in which ſuch Bondmen were to be eſteemed. And therefore I truſt I may fairly retort the obſervation of my learned friend,---- ‘ *How dangerous is it to build doctrines,*’ (that is in favour of abſolute ſlavery) ‘ *upon ſuch parallels and* ‘ *compariſons!*”

'PLE OF THE HOLY GHOST, (which
'is) *in you, which you have of God, and* YOU
'ARE NOT YOUR OWN? FOR YE ARE
'BOUGHT WITH A PRICE: *therefore glo-*
'*rify God* IN YOUR BODY, *and in your*
'*spirit*, WHICH ARE GOD'S,' (1 Cor. vi.
19, 20.) and, consequently, it is the duty of
a *Christian legislature* to vindicate THE
LORD'S FREEMEN *from* SLAVERY, as
all mankind are included in the same
inestimable purchase, for it is not only
their *souls* but even their *bodies, which
are God's ;*' and therefore it is an abominable *facriledge*, that those *bodies* which
are capable of being the ' *temple of*
' *the Holy Ghost,*' should be esteemed
the mere *chattels* and private property
of mercenary planters and merchants,
merely for the sake of a little worldly
gain!

BUT slaveholders may perhaps alledge that *believing masters* are mentioned ed as '*faithful and beloved*,' in one of the texts, which I have cited, and are also expressly accounted as '*partakers of the benefit*,' (see 1 Timothy, vi. 2.) so that, from thence, they may perhaps infer, that *slavekeeping* is not inconsistent with their Christian profession.

But these expressions are included in that part of the apostles charge to *Timothy*, which relates merely to the instruction of servants, so that there is no room to suppose, that any reference was intended to the practice of the masters by way of *justification*. The meaning therefore can amount to no more than this, viz. that, as it is the duty of servants to '*count their own masters*,' (even those that are *unbelievers*) ' wor-
' thy of ALL HONOUR ‡, THAT THE NAME OF GOD AND HIS DOCTRINE BE

---

‡ Apparently meaning, '*all honour*,' which is not inconsistent with their duty to God.

'BE NOT BLASPHEMED,' so the same reason obliges them, more especially, to count their *believing* masters '*worthy* 'of *all* (lawful) *honour*,' because of their *Christian profession*, which renders them *accepted of God*. For common charity obliges us, as Christians, to suppose that all men, who believe and hold the same profession as ourselves, are '*faithful and beloved*,' as well as '*par-*' '*takers of the benefit*' of Christ's redemption, ‡ because *Belief* is the true means of

---

‡ Christ's redemption does not seem to be '*the benefit*' spoken of in the text, though I have admitted this implication to avoid controversy. Dr. *Whitby*, supposes that *the benefit of the service* is meant, and he construes the sentence accordingly, ' *because they who par-* ' *take of the* BENEFIT OF THE SERVICE, *are faithful and* ' *beloved.*' And Dr. *George Benson*, also, renders it in the same sense, viz. ' *because they who partake of* THE ' BENEFIT OF THEIR SERVICE, *are Christians, and be-* ' *loved of God.*' And then he adds in a note, ' *This* ' (says he) *I take to have been spoken of* THE MASTERS, ' *who received the* BENEFIT OF THE SERVICE *of their* ' *slaves.* So the author of the Syriac version seems to have ' *understood*

of leading and difposing men to acquire fuch happinefs; and though many other neceffary Chriftian qualities may feem wanting in our *believing brethren*, yet we muft not prefume to condemn them; God alone being their *Judge*: and, for this reafon alfo, *Chriftian fervants* muft not condemn and defpife their *believing mafters,* (though they know themfelves *equal in dignity as brethren,* and that it is, confequently, their mafters *duty* to treat them *as brethren,)* but muft render them fervice the more willingly on this *account,* having *brotherly love* as an additional motive to *faithful fervice.* It is manifeft, therefore, that this text was intended to regulate the conduct

'underftood the words. The MS. called Pet. 2. read
'(εργασιας labor) and Pet. 3. and Borner, read ευσεβειας
'piety,' for which he refers us to Kufter's edition of Dr.
Mill, 'And finally (fays he) I would obfervethat ευεργεσια
'is never ufed, throughout the New Teftament, for the pri-
'vilege of having the gofpel or the unfpeakable BENEFIT
'of eternal life,'

conduct of *Christian servants*, and not that of *Christian masters*; for, with regard to the former, the doctrine is perfectly consistent with the other texts, that I have quoted; which is not the case when it is applied to justify the mere temporal claims of *masters* or *slaveholders*, because there are many clear and incontrovertible precepts throughout the New Testament for regulating the conduct of *Christian masters*, which exclude the *justification* of any *such claims* among Christians, and consequently forbid any application or interpretation of these particular texts in favour of them: and besides we must always remember, that it is not lawful to maintain an hypothesis upon the testimony *of any one single text of doubtful interpretation*, especially when the same does not clearly correspond with the rest of the scriptures, and cannot bear the test ʻ *of the royal law*,' of

which

which more shall be said in my tract 'on *the Law of Liberty*.'

I mention this text of St. *Paul*, as one of 'doubtful interpretation,' because commentators are divided concerning the application of the very words on which the imaginary justification of the slaveholder is supposed to be founded! Many learned men (and Dr. *Hammond* among the rest) have construed the words — 'ὅτι πιϛοι εισιν και αγαπητοι, οἱ της ευεργεσιας αντιλαμβανομενοι, (1 Tim. vi. 2,) ‡ in a very different manner from the common version, and applied them *to the servants*, which entirely destroys the presumption in favour of the slaveholder.

Nevertheless I have contented myself th the common rendering, being convinced

‡ These words are translated by Dr. *Hammond*, as follows, —— '*because they who help to do good, are faithful and beloved*,' and he uses several arguments to shew that these epithets refer *to the servants*, rather than *to the masters*.

vinced that no conclusions can fairly be drawn from this text in favour of Slavery, even when the epithets " *faithful and beloved,*" &c. are applied *to the Masters*; because the signification of them must necessarily be restrained within the bounds of *gospel doctrine*; and, therefore, we cannot conceive that the apostle intended, by the application of these epithets, to justify any practices which are inconsistent with *the benevolence* enjoined in other parts of the New Testament; for this would be liable to produce a contrary effect from that which the apostle expressly intended by his injunction, viz. that " *the name of God and his doctrine be not blasphemed.*"

Thus it appears, I hope, that the principles, on which the doctrine of the *servants submission* is founded, are clearly expressed; so that *Slaveholders* can have no right to avail themselves of any
of

of these texts to *enforce an* ABSOLUTE SUBMISSION; for, though these several texts clearly justify *the Slave,* yet they cannot justify the Master, unless he can shew that the same *principles, (or reason of the Law,)* on which they are founded, hold good also on *his* side of the question. (1) Can the Slaveholders and African

---

(1) This is apparently the case in the other " *different relations of life, mentioned in those contexts;*" as in *the relation* between *husbands* and *their wives, parents* and *their children,* but is far otherwise in the *relation* between *masters and their servants,* (unless free *hired servants* are to be understood,) and therefore the objection of my learned friend, drawn from thence, cannot be just. He says, " *If the connexion of persons in the two former respects be lawful, so that husbands had a right to the subjection of their wives, and wives a right to the love of their husbands; parents had a right to the honour and obedience of their children, and children a right to maintenance and instruction by their parents: unnatural* (says he) *is it to imagine the connection between Masters and Slaves was looked upon by him as absolutely unlawful, so that the former had no right to rule the latter! Indeed, he very clearly signifies* (says he) *that the right of dominion remained, when he opposes* " DOING WRONG TO OBEYING IN ALL THINGS " THEIR MASTERS ACCORDING TO THE FLESH, " &c.

African traders alledge, for instance, that they shall "*adorn the doctrine of* "*God*

" &c. as he does. *Coloss.* iii. 25." " Ὁ δὲ ἀδικῶν " κομιεῖται ὃ ἠδίκησεν."

But my learned friend has entirely misunderstood the purport and intention of my arguments on these several texts relating to *obedience* and *submission.* I have not attempted to prove, *by these particular expressions of the apostle,* that " *the connexion between Masters and Slaves* " *was looked upon by him as absolutely unlawful,* so that " the former had *no right to rule the latter* ;" for this I have demonstrated, I trust, by OTHER AUTHORITIES *of Scripture* equally authentic, and much less liable to be misunderstood. My attempt to explain the texts in question extends no farther than to shew that they do not really *justify the uncharitable claims of the modern Slaveholders,* though they are frequently cited for that purpose.

An attempt to shew *that any particular doctrine is* NOT NECESSARILY IMPLIED *in a certain text or texts of Scripture,* is a very different thing from an attempt to PROVE or AUTHENTICATE AN OPPOSITE DOCTRINE *by the same text of Scripture!* For instance, when my learned friend asserts, as above, that the apostle to the Colos- " sians, iii. 25. *very clearly signifies that the right of do-* " *minion remained, when he opposes* DOING WRONG TO " OBEYING *in all things their Masters,*" &c. I do not pretend to build an *opposite doctrine upon the very same words,* but shall only endeavour to shew that this supposed " *right of dominion*" is not necessarily *implied* in the text which my friend has cited in support of it.

The

" *God our Saviour,*" (Titus ii. 10.) by perſiſting in their unnatural pretenſions to

The ſervants are indeed expreſsly and plainly exhorted to *obedience* and *ſubmiſſion,* as well in this as in all the other texts before recited, ſo that a contrary behaviour in them might certainly be eſteemed a " *do-*" *ing wrong*" on their part yet this by no means implies " *a right of dominion*" veſted in the Maſter; for that would prove too much; becauſe the like ſubmiſſion is elſewhere equally enjoined to thoſe who are expreſsly ſaid to " *endure grief,* SUFFERING WRONG-" FULLY," ($\pi\alpha\sigma\chi\omega\nu$ $\alpha\delta\iota\kappa\omega\varsigma,$) and we cannot ſuppoſe (as I have before obſerved) that the *ſubmiſſion enjoined* implies a *right* in the Maſter to exerciſe ſuch a *dominion* as that of *oppreſſing others* UNJUSTLY, or $\alpha\delta\iota\kappa\omega\varsigma$; for that could not poſſibly tend to promote the declared purpoſes of the apoſtle's exhortations, viz. " *that the name of God and his doctrine be not blaſphemed,*" (1 Tim. vi.) and again, " *that they may adorn the doctrine of God in* " *all* THINGS," (Titus ii. 9.) Theſe purpoſes, however, are fully anſwered in the advice given by the ſame apoſtle to all the other *different relations of life* mentioned by my worthy friend. WIVES may " *adorn* " *the doctrine of God*" by SUBMISSION to their " *own* " *huſbands, as it is fit in the Lord.*" (See Coloſſ. iii. 18.) And HUSBANDS, by *love* to their *wives:* for they are expreſsly charged in the following verſe " *not to* " *be bitter againſt them,*" that is, they muſt, by *love* and *ſincere affection,* moderate and ſoften that ſupreme authority with which *huſbands* are entruſted, (by the laws of God and man,) that they may *rule* rather by the gentle influence of an inviolable *love* and *fidelity,*

as

to an absolute *property* in their poor *brethren?* or that they " *do the will of* " *God*

as so good an example will seldom fail to produce due *respect*, and will certainly " *adorn the doctrine*" or profession of the Christian. CHILDREN " *may adorn the* " *doctrine of God*" by OBEDIENCE *to their* " *parents in* " *all things, for this is well-pleasing* (says the text) *unto* " *the Lord.*" (v. 20.) And again, the reciprocal duty of FATHERS is plainly pointed out to be a prudent moderation of that *paternal* authority with which they are entrusted, for they are carefully warned against an arbitrary severity, " *Provoke not* (says the apostle) *your* " *children to anger, lest they be discouraged.*" SERVANTS are in the very next verse (v. 22.) commanded to " *obey in all things their Masters according to the flesh,* " *not with eye-service, as* MEN-PLEASERS, *but in* " *singleness of heart,* FEARING GOD :" so that the SUBMISSION of the servants was also to *adorn the* " *doctrine of God,*" it being manifestly enjoined only for *God's sake*, and not on account of any supposed " RIGHT OF DOMINION" invested in the *Masters*, which the following verses (v. 23, and 24.) when *applied to* THE SERVANTS, sufficiently demonstrate,——" And " *whatsoever ye do, do it heartily as to the Lord, and* " NOT UNTO MEN : *knowing, that of* THE LORD " *ye shall receive* THE REWARD OF THE INHE- " RITANCE: *for* YE SERVE THE LORD CHRIST." And to the same eternal and unerring Dispenser of *Rewards* (and not to *temporal Masters)* is attributed the power of punishing the " *doing wrong,*" mentioned in the very next verse ; which, according to my learned friend's notion, is *opposed* to *obeying in all things the*

Masters

"*God from the heart*," (Ephesians vi. 5, &c.) when they retain their *neighbour*

Masters;—" *he that* DOETH WRONG (says the text) *shall receive for* THE WRONG *which he hath done: and* THERE IS NO RESPECT OF PERSONS." (v. 25.)

Such strict *impartiality* in the administration of justice cannot always be attributed, with certainty, even to the best-regulated *human* tribunal, and much less is it applicable to the decisions of uncontrouled *will* and *pleasure*, in punishing " *wrong doing*," under the absolute *dominion* of Slaveholders! No earthly *dominion* whatever is conducted with such an equal distribution of *rewards* and *punishments*, as that it may always with truth be said, " *there is no respect of persons*," for this is the proper characteristic of the *judgements and dominion* of GOD and CHRIST alone. " *For* THE LORD *is* JUDGE, *and with him is* NO RESPECT OF PERSONS." Ecclesiasticus xxxv. 12. " *For there is* NO RESPECT OF PERSONS *with* GOD." Rom. ii. 11. And, therefore, we may fairly conclude that the punishment, not only of SLAVES, but that also of MASTERS, that " *do wrong*," is to be understood in the text which my friend has cited to support his notion of a " *right of dominion*" vested in the *Masters*; so that the said supposed *right* has, indeed, but a very " *slippery*" foundation! Agreeable to my last remark on this text, (Coloss. iii. 24.) the learned Dr. Whitby has commented upon it, as if he thought it exactly parallel to another declaration of the same apostle, (viz. Ephes. vi. 8 and 9.) wherein not only both *Masters* and *Servants* are unquestionably included, but also the *dominion*, or *judgement*, in *which* " THERE IS NO RESPECT

" OF

bour in an involuntary unrewarded servitude for life? If they can do this, I shall

"OF PERSONS," is expresly attributed to our "MAS-
"TER IN HEAVEN."—"*Chrift, in judging men at*
"*the laft day,* (fays the Doctor,) *will have* NO RESPECT
"*to the quality or external condition of any man's perfon;*
"*but,* WHETHER HE BE BOND OR FREE, *he fhall*
"*receive recompence* FOR THE GOOD THAT HE HATH
"DONE, *in obedience to him; whether he be* MASTER *or*
"SERVANT, *he fhall be punifhed for* THE WRONG THAT
"HE DOTH *in thofe relations.*"

If all thefe circumftances be duly confidered, it will manifeftly appear, I truft, that the Mafters fuppofed "*right of dominion*" (which, certainly, is *not* EXPRESSED in the text) cannot even be *implied* in thefe contexts, nor in any of the parallel paffages already recited! Can the Mafter *adorn the* "*doctrine of* "*God our Saviour,*" (as in the other indiffoluble relations of life,) by continuing the unnatural *connection* of *Mafter* and *Slave,* and by *exacting* involuntary labour from his *brethren, without wages* or *reward,* agreeable to my friend's notions of the fuppofed implied "*right* "*of dominion?*" The reciprocal duty of the Mafter is mentioned, indeed, in the next chapter, (Col. iv. 1.) but it is of fuch a nature as muft neceffarily lead Chriftian Mafters to abhor any fuch fuppofed "*right of* "*dominion*" as that which is tolerated in the Britifh colonies, and which my friend feems defirous to defend! The *Mafters* are not directed by the apoftle to claim as their own, by "*right of dominion,*" the *labour* of their fervants WITHOUT WAGES, but, on the contrary, are expresly commanded to "GIVE *unto* (their) *fer*
"*vants*

shall have reason to be silent. But if, on the contrary, it should evidently appear

" *wants that which is* JUST *and* EQUAL;" which comprehends (as I have fully shewn in the preceding tract) such a measure of *generosity, recompence,* and *benevolence,* on the part of *the Master,* as is totally inconsistent with the claims and views of modern *Slaveholders!* and, if put in practice, would necessarily effect the entire abolition of slavery!

The Masters are likewise carefully reminded, in the last mentioned text, that they " *also have a Master* " *in Heaven.*" (Col. iv. 1)—A *Master,* by whose example they are bound to regulate their conduct, so that this consideration alone is a sufficient antidote against *slavery*; for the principal doctrine of *that heavenly Master* was LOVE, which cannot subsist with the contrary *exaction of involuntary servitude!* " *This is my* " *commandment,*" (said that glorious and gracious MASTER,) " *That ye* LOVE *one another* AS *I have* LOVED *you.*" The nature of *his love* (which we are to imitate, that is, to LOVE *as he hath* LOVED *us)* is then immediately described as exceeding all bounds of comparison, " *Greater* LOVE" (said he) " *hath* " *no man than this, that a man lay down his life for his* " FRIENDS. *Ye are my* FRIENDS, *if ye do whatsoever* " *I command you.* HENCEFORTH I CALL YOU NOT " SERVANTS." Here is an express *enfranchisement* of *his Servants* for our example! The universal *Lord* and *Master* of all men delights in promoting *the dignity of human nature;* which cannot be said of the temporal *Slaveholder,* who enforces an imaginary " *right of dominion,*" by exacting an *involuntary service,* and that

for

pear that a *very different behaviour* is required of *Christian Masters,* " that
" the

for no other purpose than for the sake of a little pecuniary gain, by depriving the *labourer of his hire*; which savours of no other *love* but *self-love*; whereas, our disinterested Lord and Master hath even *laid down his life* through *love* and *compassion* to his SERVANTS, and hath *declared us free,* as before recited. — " Henceforth I call you not SERVANTS; *for the Servant*" (said he) " *knoweth not what his Lord doeth; but I have called you* FRIENDS; *for all things that I have heard of my Father I have made known unto you:*" (John xv. 12–15.) And, in the 17th verse, he again enforces his doctrine of LOVE: " *These things I command you,* (said he,) *that ye* LOVE *one another.*" The measure of this indispensible LOVE is expresly declared in the Scriptures, " *Thou shalt* LOVE *thy neighbour* AS THYSELF. " LOVE *worketh no ill to his neighbour: therefore* LOVE " (is) *the fulfilling of the law.*" (Rom. xiii. 9 and 10.)

Such LOVE, therefore, is clearly incompatible with the arbitrary claims of the Slaveholder, who can neither be *said* to LOVE *his neighbour as himself,* nor to cherish that LOVE *which worketh no ill to his neighbour,* whilst he strenuously contends for such " *a right of* " *dominion*" as may enable him to exact, not only the *involuntary* service of his *neighbours* and *brethren,* contrary to the law of nature, but also to rob them of the *fruits of their own labours,* " GIVING THEM NOT " FOR THEIR WORK;" against which practices a severe denunciation of WOE is expresly declared in the Scriptures; as I have fully demonstrated in my tract on " *the Law of Retribution,*" as well as in the preceding

"*the name of God and his doctrine be
"*not blasphemed*," (1 Tim. vi. 1.) they
must be obliged to allow that the "*reason, or life of the law*" is against them;
and, consequently, that none of these
texts, relating to Christian servants, are
capable of affording them the least excuse for their selfish pretensions. They
will find also, upon a more careful examination of the Scriptures, that they
themselves are as much bound by the gospel to bear personal injuries with patience
and humility, as their Slaves. Because
the benevolent principles of the *gospel
of peace* require all men, *freemen* as *well
as slaves*, to return "*good for evil.*"
"*Bless them that* CURSE *you*," (said our
Lord,)

ding tract: and, therefore, as it is necessary to con-
strue difficult or dubious passages of *Scripture* consistently with the general tenour of *Scripture* evidence,
it would be highly improper to admit this *opposite doctrine* of a supposed "RIGHT OF DOMINION," especially as the same *is not expressed* in the text which my
learned friend has cited for it, but is merely drawn
forth by an imaginary *implication!*

Lord,) "*and* PRAY *for them which* DE-
"SPITEFULLY USE YOU. *And unto*
"*him that* SMITETH *thee on the one*
"*cheek, offer alſo the other;* and him
"*that* TAKETH AWAY *thy cloke, for-*
"*bid not* (to take thy) *coat alſo,*" &c.
Luke vi. 28, 29. But, though *ſubmiſſion* and *placability* are thus unqueſti-
onably enjoined to the *ſufferers* in all
the caſes above recited in the text, yet
ſurely no reaſonable man will pretend
to alledge, from thence, that *tyrants* and
oppreſſors have thereby obtained a legal
right, under the goſpel, to *curſe others,*
and uſe them *deſpitefully;* or that the
unjuſt oppreſſion of *ſtrikers and robbers*
is thereby authorized or juſtified! In the
ſame light exactly muſt we view the *Slave-
holders* claim of *private property in the
perſons of men,* whenever an attempt is
made to ſupport it on the foundation of
any ſuch texts as I have quoted, wherein
ſervants or ſlaves are exhorted to ſubmit

with

with passive obedience, &c. to their Masters; because the *right* (as it is improperly called) or pretension of the Master may with the greatest propriety be compared to the pretended *right* or authority of oppressing or robbing others, which is too often exercised by imperial tyrants and despotic princes, as well as by *their brethren in iniquity* of a lower class, viz. pirates, highwaymen, and extortioners of every degree! The gospel of peace cannot authorize the oppression of these lawless men, though it clearly enjoins patience, submission, and acquiescence, to the individuals that are enjured, whether freemen or slaves! The *placability* and *absolute submission*, commanded by the last-cited text, to Christians *in general*, are manifestly founded on the very same principles with that *particular* submission which the gospel requires of *Christian slaves*; and is farther parallel to the latter, by being *equally*

qually passive; so that the *oppression* of the *Slaveholder* can no more be justified by any text of the New Testament, that I am able to find, than the *oppression* of the *striker* and *robber*.

Unhappily for the Christian world, the duties of *patience, submission,* and *placability,* enjoined by the gospel to *persons injured,* are too commonly either misunderstood or rejected; though the *temporal,* as well as the *eternal,* happiness of mankind greatly depends upon a conscientious and proper observation of these duties: for even the most rigid obedience to the letter of the command would be far from being productive, either of the *real evils* to which the pernicious doctrine of *a national passive obedience* apparently tends, or of the *imaginary inconveniences* apprehended by the advocates for *duelling,* because the same benevolent principles, (viz. universal love and charity,

charity, founded on the great commandment, "Thou shalt love thy neighbour as thyself,") which oblige the true Christian, most *disinterestedly*, to forgive all injuries, and pass over every affront offered to his *own person*, will necessarily engage him, on the other hand, as *disinterestedly*, to oppose every degree of oppression and injustice, which affects his *brethren and neighbours*, when he has a fair opportunity of assisting them; and from hence arises the zeal of good men for *just* and *equitable laws*, as being the most effectual means of preserving the *peace* and *happiness* of the community, by curbing the insolence and violence of wicked men. We have an eminent example of this *loyal zeal* in the behaviour of the apostle Paul, who could not brook an infringement of *the Roman liberty* from any persons whatever in the administration of government, though he could endure *personal injuries* from

from men unconnected therewith, and the perfecutions of the multitude, with all the *Christian patience* and *meekness* which the gofpel requires. The Scripture-hiftory of this great apoftle affords many proofs of his extraordinary humility and patience *under sufferings,* fo that his fpirited oppofition to the illegal proceedings of magiftrates cannot be attributed to *private refentment* on his own account, but merely to his zeal for *the public good,* founded upon the great Chriftian principle of " *loving his neigh-* " *bour as himfelf,*" fince the maintaining of *good laws* is, certainly, the moft effectual means of promoting the welfare and happinefs of fociety. His refolute and free cenfure of the magiftrates at Philippi, in the meffage which he fent by their own ferjeants, (2) his fpirited re-

---

(2) " And, when it was day, the magiftrates fent the
" ferjeants, faying, Let thofe men go. And the keeper
" of the prifon told this, faying to Paul, The ma-
" giftrates

remonstrance to the chief captain at Jerusalem, (3) and his severe rebuke to

"giſtrates have ſent to let you go: now therefore de-
"part, and go in peace. But Paul ſaid unto them,
"*They have beaten us openly uncondemned, being Romans,*
"*and have caſt* (us) *into priſon: and now do they thruſt*
"*us out privily? nay verily;* but *let them come themſelves*
"*and fetch us out.* And the ſerjeants told theſe
"words unto the magiſtrates: and they feared when
"they heard that they were Romans. And they came
"and beſought them, and brought *(them)* out, and
"deſired *(them)* to depart out of the city." Acts
xvi. 35 to 39.

(3) "The chief captain commanded him to be
"brought into the caſtle, and bade that he ſhould be
"examined by ſcourging; that he might know where-
"fore they cried ſo againſt him. And, as they bound
"him with thongs, Paul ſaid unto the centurion that
"ſtood by, *Is it lawful for you to ſcourge a man that*
"*is a Roman, and uncondemned?* When the centurion
"heard *(that)*, he went and told the chief captain,
"ſaying, Take heed what thou doeſt: for this man
"is a Roman. Then the chief captain came, and ſaid
"unto him, Tell me, art thou a Roman? he ſaid,
"Yea. And the chief captain anſwered, With a great
"ſum obtained I this freedom, and Paul ſaid, But I
"was free born. Then ſtraightway they departed
"from him which ſhould have examined him: *and the*
"*chief captain was alſo afraid after he knew that he*
"*was*

to the high prieſt himſelf, even on the ſeat of judgement, (4) are remarkable inſtances of this obſervation.

In the laſt-mentioned inſtance, indeed, the apoſtle was charged, by thoſe "*that ſtood by,*" with *reviling God's high*

" *was a Roman, and becauſe he had bound him.* On
" the morrow, becauſe he would have known the cer-
" tainty wherefore he was accuſed of the Jews, he
" looſed him from *(his)* bands, and commanded the
" chief prieſts and all their council to appear, and
" brought Paul down, and ſet him before them."
Acts xxii. 24 to 30.

(4) " And Paul earneſtly beholding the council,
" ſaid, Men and brethren, I have lived in all good
" conſcience before God until this day. And the
" high prieſt Ananias commanded them that ſtood by
" him to ſmite him on the mouth. Then Paul ſaid
" unto him, *God ſhall ſmite thee*, (thou) WHITED
" WALL; *for, ſitteſt thou to judge me after the law, and*
" *commandeſt me to be ſmitten contrary to the law?* And
" they that ſtood by ſaid, Revileſt thou God's high
" prieſt? Then ſaid Paul, 1 wiſt not, brethren, that
" he was the high prieſt, for it is written, Thou ſhalt
" not ſpeak evil of the ruler of thy people." Acts
xxiii. 1 to 5.

high priest, which would have been a notorious breach of the law, had there not been circumstances of justification sufficient to vindicate the severity of the Apostle's censure: these, however, were not urged by the apostle himself, who best knew how to behave towards those with whom he had to do. He readily allowed the principle (however) on which the censure of his accusers was founded, but he by no means retracted what he had so justly applied to the person of the unworthy magistrate *who sat to judge him*; neither did he even *acknowledge* him to be the *high priest,* though he was expressly questioned for a supposed misbehaviour to that dignitary! His answer was cautiously worded.— He did not say, —— *I knew not that this person, whom I have censured, was the high priest,* but, —— ουκ ηδειν, αδελφοι, οτι εςιν αρχιερευς, *&c.* " *I knew* " *not, brethren, that there is a high* " *priest.*"

"*priest.*" (5) Which anſwer, though on the firſt hearſay it ſeems to bear ſome affinity to an excuſe or apology for what had paſt, yet, in reality, includes a ſtill farther rebuke; for it plainly implies that the *high prieſt,* in whoſe preſence the apoſtle then ſtood, was (in ſome reſpect or other) deficient or blameable in his deportment as chief magiſtrate, either that he did not duly ſupport the dignity of that ſacred and diſtinguiſhing public character, ſo that he did not ſeem to be *high prieſt,* and of courſe could not be known and honoured as ſuch; or elſe that his behaviour had been ſo unjuſt and illegal that he did not deſerve to be conſidered as a *lawful magiſtrate,* who had publicly demeaned himſelf

---

(5) The learned Hugh Broughton has conſtrued the text as follows,— " *I knewe not, brethren, that there* " *was a high prieſt ;*" but the words, ουκ ηδειν, αδελφοι, οτι εϛιν αρχιερευς, are more literally rendered above. CASTALIO reads it,— " *Neſciebam, fratres, eſſe pontificem.*"—And HEINSIUS,—" *Summum eſſe ſacerdotem* " *ignorabam.*"

himself as *a tyrant*, by commanding a prisoner to be beaten, *contrary to law*, without hearing his defence! And, that this latter sense is most probable we may learn by the following circumstance, viz. that the apostle chose to decline the dispute, and to wave the accusation about *reviling the high priest*, by *acknowledging* the principle of law on which it was manifestly founded, viz. *Thou shalt not speak evil of the ruler of thy people*. But, be pleased to observe, he neither *acknowledged* that he himself had broken the said precept by so severely censuring the unjust *ruler*, nor did he *acknowledge* the presence of *a high priest* in the person of Ananias; neither did he allow the by-standers time enough to criticise upon the true literal meaning of his reply, (whereby they would probably have been led to demand some express recantation of the *personal* censure which he had so amply bestowed

bestowed upon the high priest,) but he prudently changed the subject in debate from *the* PERSON *of the high priest* (who was a zealous overbearing SADDUCEE) (6) to an avowed *censure of his whole sect*, charging the SADDUCEES in particular with the unjust persecution, then before the assembly, and openly appealing to the opposite party, *the Pharisees*, in order to divide his united enemies: " *I* " *am a* PHARISEE, (said he,) *the son* " *of a* PHARISEE; *of the hope and re-* " *surrection of the dead I* AM CALLED " IN QUESTION." Such a manifest reflection against the whole body of Sadducees

(6) Ὁ δὲ νεώτερος ΑΝΑΝΟΣ, ὃν τὴν ἀρχιερωσυνην ἐφαμεν παρειληφεναι, θρασυς ἠν τον τροπον, και τολμητης δ.αφεροντως. Αἱρεσιν δε μετηει την ΣΑΔΔΟΥΚΑΙΩΝ, οἱπερ εισι περι τας κρισεις ωμοι παρα πανλας τους Ιουδαιους, καθως ηδη δεδηλωκαμεν· ἀτε δη εν τοιουτος ων ὁ ΑΝΑΝΟΣ, &c. But the younger ANANUS, who, as we have said, obtained the pontificate, was of a bold and daring disposition, and followed the sect of the SADDUCEES, who, with respect to judgements, are more cruel than all the rest of the Jews, as we have already demonstrated. Therefore, Ananias being of this stamp, &c.

Sadducees cannot by any means favour the suppofition of an intended apology, or recantation, in the preceding fentence, to foothe the enraged leader of that very party, whom he had publicly branded as a hypocrite, with the fignificant appellation of *whited wall!* Let it be alfo remembered that the fuppofed breach of the precept ("*thou fhalt not fpeak evil of* "*the* RULER *of thy people*") could not reft entirely on the circumftance of KNOWING ANANIAS TO BE THE HIGH PRIEST; for, whether the apoftle *did know*, or *did not know*, that Ananias was *high prieft*, yet he certainly *knew*, before he cenfured him, that he was *a ruler of the people*, and that he then fat in *the quality of a judge;* (for this is declared in the very cenfure itfelf, — "*fitteft thou to* JUDGE ME *after the* "*law, and commandeft me to be fmitten* CONTRARY TO LAW?") fo that whether *Ananias* was really *high prieft*, or or not, yet he was manifeftly cenfured in his official capacity as a *ruler*, or *magiftrate*, and not as a private individual, through any inadvertency or miftake of the apoftle, as fome commentators have conceived. And, even when the apoftle was informed, by thofe " *that ftood by*," that the magiftrate whom he had cenfured was the *high prieft*, *(" revileft thou God's high prieft?")* Yet his reply, *(" I knew not, brethren, that there is a high prieft,")* when fairly compared with the preceding cenfure of Ananias, as an *unjuft* dipenfer of God's law, *(" fitteft thou to judge me according to law?* &c.) proves, as I before remarked, that the apoftle neither acknowledged the dignity of *a high prieft*, nor that of a *legal ruler, in the perfon of Ananias*, though he knew him at the fame time TO BE A RULER, and had cenfured him as fuch, for having notorioufly proftituted the power and authority

rity of a *ruler*, and violated the law, by commanding him to be *stricken contrary to law*, notwithstanding, that *he sat to judge* (as the apostle remarked) "AC-"CORDING *to the law;*" in which case no epithet whatever could be so apt and expressive to mark the true character of the dignified hypocrite in power, as *whited wall!* This proves, that the apostle knew well enough with whom he had to do. The censure was too just, and his prophecy in the accomplishment too true, *("God shall smite thee,"* thou *whited wall,)* (7) to be esteemed a mere unguarded sally of resentment! The latter supposition is, indeed, inconsistent with the remarkable *sagacity, prudence,* and *readiness* of *mind*, which always distinguished

(7) This denunciation of God's vengeance against Ananias was fully justified by the event; for, Josephus (as the learned monsieur Martin remarks) reports that he was killed in Jerusalem with his brother Ezechias. " Josephe rapporte," liv. 2. de la guerre des Juifs, " qu'il fut massacré dans Jérusalem avec son frère " Ezéchias."

guished this apostle in bearing his testimony to the truth, on the most dangerous emergences! The apostle's known character as *a chosen vessel* for Christ's service, and as an exemplary preacher of RIGHTEOUSNESS, will by no means permit us to conceive that he was either guilty of any *mistake* or *inadvertency* with respect to *the person* of the high priest on this occasion; or of any *illegal* or misbecoming behaviour to him as a *ruler* or *judge* of the people! When these several circumstances are compared with the general bad character of Ananias, (8) as

(8) This malicious Sadducee very soon afterwards gave so flagrant a proof of his injustice and cruelty towards the Christians, that even the *Jewish historian*, Josephus, has recorded it as an event which gave offence to all good and loyal men at that time in Jerusalem; I mean the murder of the apostle James, bishop of Jerusalem, whom Josephus stiles *the brother of Jesus, who was called Christ*. The Jewish historian, therein, bears a remarkable testimony in favour of Christianity, — Ἅτε δη ων τοιυτος ων ὁ Ανανος, (for he is described, in the preceding quotation from Josephus, as a bold daring man of the most cruel sect,) νομισας εχειν καιρον. επιτηδειον,

δια

as a persecuting zealot of the most virulent and intolerant sect among the Jews, it must appear that the apostle accounted that person unworthy of any esteem as a magistrate, whom he had so publicly convicted

διὰ τὸ τεθνάναι μὲν Φῆςον, Ἀλβῖνον δὲ ἔτι κατὰ τὴν ὁδὸν ὑπάρχειν, καθίζει συνέδριον κριτῶν, καὶ παραγαγὼν εἰς αὐτὸ ΤΟΝ ΑΔΕΛΦΟΝ ΙΗΣΟΥ ΤΟΥ ΛΕΓΟΜΕΝΟΥ ΧΡΙΣΤΟΥ, ΙΑΚΩΒΟΣ ὄνομα αὐτῷ, καί τινας ἑτέρους, ὡς παρανομησάντων κατηγορίαν ποιησάμενος, παρέδωκε λευσθησομένους· ὅσοι δὲ ἐδόκουν ἐπιεικέστατοι τῶν κατὰ τὴν πόλιν εἶναι, καὶ περὶ τοὺς νόμους ἀκριβεῖς, βαρέως ἤνεγκαν ἐπὶ τούτῳ, καὶ πέμπουσιν πρὸς τὸν βασιλέα κρυφα παρακαλοῦντες αὐτὸν ἐπιστεῖλαι τῷ Ἀνάνῳ, μηκέτι τοιαῦτα πράσσειν, μηδὲ γὰρ τὸ πρῶτον ὀρθῶς αὐτὸν πεποιηκέναι. Which is translated by Mr. Whiston as follows,—— "*When, therefore, Ananus was*
"*of this disposition, he thought he had now a proper oppor-*
"*tunity* (to exercise his authority). Festus *was*
"*dead; and* Albinus *was but upon the road. So he*
"*assembled the sanhedrim of judges, and brought before*
"*them* THE BROTHER OF JESUS, WHO WAS CALLED
"CHRIST, *whose name was* JAMES, *and some others,*
"(or some of his companions,) *and when he had formed*
"*an accusation against them as breakers of the law, he de-*
"*livered them to be stoned. The* MOST EQUITABLE OF
"THE CITIZENS, AND SUCH AS WERE THE MOST
"UNEASY AT THE BREACH OF THE LAWS, DIS-
"LIKED WHAT WAS DONE. *They also sent to the*
"*king,* (Agrippa,) *desiring him to send to* Ananus,
"*that he should act so no more; for that what he had*
"*already done was not to be justified.*"

victed of abusing and perverting the legal authority with which he had been entrusted; and, indeed, a notorious breach of the law, by any man in the capacity of *a ruler*, may reasonably be esteemed a temporary disqualification for such an honourable trust; for, a *judge* without *justice* and *righteousness*, who openly perverts judgement, does thereby unquestionably degrade himself from the dignity of his station, and render himself unworthy, for the time being, of that respect which is otherwise due to his rank in office. The same apostle, indeed, upon another occasion, commands us to give " *honour to whom honour" is due*; but what *honour* can be due to a convicted hypocrite, — a " *whited* " *wall*,"— a " *wolf in sheep's cloath-* " *ing*,"—to an " *Ananias on the seat* " *of judgement?*" Such characters must expect such treatment, as *Ananias* met with, from all sensible and discerning men;

men; if the latter are also equally *loyal* with the apostle, I mean in the strict and proper sense of the word *loyal*, (which is so frequently misapplied and perverted by sycophants,) that is, if they are equally zealous with that apostle for *law*, *justice*, and *righteousness*, for the general good of mankind! So that if we approve of the apostle's advice, in the beginning of the same sentence, viz. " RENDER, THEREFORE, " UNTO ALL THEIR DUES,"—" *tri-* " *bute, unto whom tribute,"*—" *custom,* " *to whom custom,"*—" FEAR, *to whom* " FEAR,"—" HONOUR *to whom* HO- " NOUR;" we must needs also allow, that the apostle's *practice* (even in his behaviour to *Ananias*) was strictly consistent with his own declared *precepts*, and that he most justly *rendered* to *Ananias* HIS DUE, when he so severely reprimanded his conduct *as a judge!* When all these circumstances are duly considered,

considered, the meaning of the apostle's reply, may, fairly enough, be paraphrased in the words of LORINUS, (9) H as

---

(9) "*Nesciebam eum esse* PONTIFICEM, *quia, ex modo loquendi furioso, non videtur esse* PONTIFEX, sed TYRANNUS." Many of the most learned and celebrated commentators have considered the apostle's censure nearly in the same light. In the learned commentary, commonly called Assembly's Annotations, the same sense is applied to the apostle's reply to the charge of having *reviled God's high priest,* viz. "*I knew him not to be a lawful high priest,* WHO THUS VIOLATETH THE LAW; and, indeed," (says the Commentary,) "*he was but an usurper.* — For proof of which they refer us to " Josephus, Ant. l. 20. c. 3. 5. " Chr. Helvic. Theat. Hist. Anno Christi, 46."

The learned MATHIAS FLACIUS FRANCOWITZ remarks, that the famous *Augustine,* bishop of Hippo, thought this reply of the apostle IRONICAL, * "*and truly,* (says he,) *it borders upon* IRONY; *for, when he saw him* (Ananias) *sit in the chief place among the priests, to judge according to the law, he necessarily* "*knew*

---

* "IRONIAM esse putat Augustinus. Est sane quiddam vicinum ironiæ. Cum enim videret eum federe inter sacerdotes loco præcipuo, et secundum legem judicare; necessariò scivit eum esse pontificem: tametsi et alioqui etiam minimi pueri necessariò id illic vel ex sola ejus pompa et asseclis vulgoque jactatis vocibus sciverunt, nedum Paulus homo tam vigilans et diligens. Sensus ergo est: Ego *non agnosco in hoc homine pontificem Dei: sed hypocritam, seductorem, et veritatis persecutorem.* Alioqui bene scio principi maledicendum non esse."

as I find him quoted by CORNELIUS A LAPIDE, viz. "*I knew not that he was*

"*knew him to be the high priest: for even the little
children knew that by his mere pomp and attendants;
and much less could a man, so watchful and diligent
as Paul, be ignorant of it; the sense therefore, is,*" (says
the learned Francowitz,) "*I do not acknowledge, in this
man, the high priest of God*, but a hypocrite, a deceiver, and a persecutor of the truth. Otherwise,
I well know that *a ruler* is not to be spoken against
or reviled.*" To the same effect, also, the learned
monsieur Martin, — "*as St. Paul*" (says he †) "*was
not ignorant, nor could be ignorant, that this was
the high priest, especially as he saw him at the head of
the sanhedrim, it is better to translate the term of the
original, by I* DID NOT THINK, *&c. as in Mark* ix.
*6. and so to understand this reply of St. Paul as a
grave and strong irony, by which he would make those
understand, by whom he was accused of the want of
respect for the high priest, that this person was a man
unworthy of that character, and that he did not believe, that a vicious and wicked man, such as Ananias, who*

† Comme St. Paul n'ignoroit pas, et ne pouvoit pas même ignorer, que ce ne fût le souverain sacrificateur, puis qu'il le voyoit à la tête du sanhédrin, il vaut miéux traduire le term de l'original par *je ne pensois pas*, comme Marc ix. 6. et prendre ainsi cette répartie de St. Paul comme une grave et forte ironie, par laquelle il vouloit fair sentir à ceux qui l'avoient repris de manquer de respect pour le souverain sacrificateur, que c'étoit un homme indigne de ce caractère ; et qu'il ne croyoit pas qu'un vicieux et un impie, comme étoit Ananias, qui avoit usurpé le pontificat en l'achetant des Romains, méritat d'être regardé comme *le souverain sacrificateur de Dieu*.

"*was the high priest*, because, from his furious manner of speaking, he did not seem to be a HIGH PRIEST, but a TYRANT." This sense is strictly consonant to *reason* and *natural right!*

Justice and *righteousness* are so inseparably connected with the proper character of a CHIEF MAGISTRATE or RULER, that any notorious perversion of those necessary principles, in the actual exercise of that official power with which

---

"*who had usurped the pontificate by purchasing it of the Romans, could deserve to be esteemed as the high priest of God!*"

It would be tedious to quote all the authorities that may be found to this purpose; the evidence, however, of the learned Dr. Whitby, as it includes more authorities than his own, is worthy the readers notice.—
" Dr. LIGHTFOOT *and* GROTIUS (says he) *think as I do, that St. Paul does* NOT *go about* TO EXCUSE HIS MISTAKE, *but rather saith, I* KNOW WELL ENOUGH THAT GOD'S HIGH PRIEST IS NOT TO BE REVILED, *but that this* ANANIAS *is a* HIGH PRIEST, *I know not, i. e. I* DO NOT OWN HIM AS SUCH *who hath procured this title by bribery: our celebrated* RABBINS *having declared that such an one is* NEITHER A JUDGE, *nor* TO BE HONOURED AS SUCH," &c.

which a magistrate is entrusted for *legal* (and not for illegal) purposes, must unavoidably distinguish the *contemptible hypocrite*, THE WHITED WALL, from the honourable MAGISTRATE, and deprive the former of the respect which is due only to the latter! " *Sittest thou to* " *judge me* ACCORDING TO THE LAW, " *and commandest me to be smitten* CON- " TRARY TO LAW?" Thus the apostle clearly explained the fitness and propriety of the reproachful figure of speech, *(whited wall,)* by which he had expressed the true character of the unworthy judge!

An appellation similar to this was given, even by our Lord himself, to *the Scribes and Pharisees,* who were the teachers and magistrates of the people: " *Wo unto you,* SCRIBES *and* PHARI- " SEES, HYPOCRITES; *for ye are like* " *unto* WHITED SEPULCHRES, *which,*
" *indeed,*

" *indeed, appear beautiful outward, but*
" *are within full of dead mens bones*
" *and of all uncleanness.*" (Matth. xxiii.
27.)—And, in the context, he calls
them " *blind guides,*" (v. 24.)—" *hypo-*
" *crites,*" (v. 25.)—" *full of hypocrisy and*
" *iniquity,*" (v. 28.)—" *partakers in the*
" *blood of the prophets,*" (v. 30.)—" *ser-*
" *pents,*"—" *generation of vipers,*"—
" *how can ye escape the damnation of hell?*"
&c. (v. 33.) Nay, Herod himself, the
tetrarch of Galilee, was not exempt-
ed from the severity of our Lord's censure, when there was a proper occasion to declare it; for, though our Lord
lived, for the most part, under Herod's
temporal jurisdiction, that is, in GALI-
LEE, yet he openly characterised the *craf-*
ty, base, and *self-interested,* disposition
of the TETRARCH, by expressly calling him *a* FOX,—(10) " *Go ye, and tell*
" *that*

(10) " The message, our Lord here sends to Herod," (says a sensible and learned commentator, the Rev. Mr. Francis

"*that* FOX," &c. (Luke xiii. 32.) and, though our Lord endured the moſt provoking

Francis Fox, in his edition of the New Teſtament, with references ſet under the text in words at length,) " *is no breach of that command which forbids the* " SPEAKING EVIL OF THE RULER OF THE PEOPLE, " *and conſequently is no blemiſh* (ſays he) *in our Lord's ex-* " *ample.* For our Lord here acts AS A PROPHET, *as* " *one who had received an extraordinary commiſſion from* " *God: and thoſe, who were truly* PROPHETS, *were, in* " *the* EXECUTION *of their* COMMISSION, *above the* " *greateſt* MEN *and moſt powerful princes, whom they* " *were not to ſpare when God ſent them to reprove for ſin.*" All this is certainly true with reſpect to the real authority of Chriſt to cenſure Herod, and that his applying ſo harſh and ſevere an expreſſion to the tetrarch " *is* " *no blemiſh in our Lord's example:*" but yet this is not, I apprehend, the proper method of reconciling the ſeeming difficulty, which ariſes from this example, of our Lord's applying a ſevere and reproachful epithet to a chief *ruler*, (in calling Herod a FOX,) when it is compared with that precept of the law, which forbids the *ſpeaking evil of the ruler of the people*; for, though our Lord had ample ſuperiority and authority to reprove whomſoever he pleaſed, even the greateſt *ruler* upon earth, yet, with reſpect to *his own perſonal behaviour*, as *a man* among *men,* he claimed no authority to diſpenſe with the poſitive precepts of the Moſaic law, on account of his own real dignity, or ſuperiority over the reſt of mankind, but ſtrictly obeyed the law in all things, and publicly declared his ſtrict conformity thereto. " *Think not,*" (ſaid he,) " *that*
" *I*

provoking indignities from the licentious soldiery and reviling multitude, *in silence*, answering not *a word*, agreeable to that striking character of a suffering Messiah,

" *I come to destroy the* LAW *or the* PROPHETS: *I am not come to destroy, but to fulfill.*" Matth v. 17.

" *By* THE LAW AND THE PROPHETS" (says the same ingenious commentator above cited) " *are meant the great rules of life, delivered in the writings of* MOSES *and the* PROPHETS, *or in the Old Testament, more especially the duties of the* MORAL *or* NATURAL LAW;" (from whence those, respecting our behaviour to RULERS, cannot with propriety be excluded;) " *These,* our Lord assures us, HE DID NOT COME *to* DESTROY *or* DISSOLVE: *It was not his design to* FREE *men from the obligation they were under to practise the* MORAL LAWS *of* GOD, *but to fulfil and perfect them. This our Lord did,* BY LIVING UP TO THOSE LAWS HIMSELF," (which totally excludes the idea of his dispensing, on account of his own real superiority, with that *moral* law respecting behaviour to rulers,) " *and becoming thereby* AN EXAMPLE TO US, *by freeing them from the corrupt glosses, which the teachers among the Jews put upon them, and by expounding them in their fullest sense, and according to their just latitude, shewing that they command not only an* OUTWARD OBEDIENCE, *but* THE OBEDIENCE *even of the* MIND *and* THOUGHTS, *as appears in what our Lord delivers in the following verses: — These laws have their foundation in the reason and nature of things, and therefore their obligation will never cease.*"

Messiah, so minutely described, many ages before, by the prophet Isaiah; (11) yet he made an apparent distinction between the VIOLENCE *and* INJUSTICE of these, as *individuals*, and the INJUSTICE of a man in a *public character*, as a *chief magistrate*; for even, in our Lord's state of extreme humiliation, when his hour of sufferings was come, he did not fail to rebuke *the* INJUSTICE of the *high priest* in his judicial capacity, because, instead of proceeding against him by the legal method of *examination by witnesses*, he had attempted to draw out matter of accusation from his own mouth, against himself, by INTERROGATORIES, according to the baneful method of arbitrary courts!

But,

---

(11) " *He was oppressed, and he was afflicted,* YET HE OPENED NOT HIS MOUTH: *he is brought as a lamb to the slaughter; and, as a sheep before her shearers* IS DUMB, SO HE OPENED NOT HIS MOUTH. *He was taken from prison, and from judgement: and who shall declare his generation? for he was cut off out of the land of the living: for the transgression of my people was he stricken!*" Isaiah liii. 7, 8.

But our Lord foon put a ftop to his impertinent QUESTIONS, by referring him to the legal method of finding evidence by witneffes: — *Why* ASKEST *" thou me?* ASK *them which heard me, " what I have faid unto them: behold, " they know what I faid."* John xviii. 21. Upon which, a time-ferving officer, who probably had not accuftomed himfelf to diftinguifh the different degrees of refpect that are due to *good* and *bad* magiftrates, " *gave Jefus a* " *blow, or rap with a rod,*" (εδωκε ῥαπισμα τω Ιησȣ,) faying, " *Anfwereft thou the* " *high prieft fo?*" (v. 22.) which open injuftice, to a perfon uncondemned, (even while he ftood in the prefence of the magiftrate, who ought to have protected him,) drew a farther *remonftrance*, even from the meekeft and humbleft man that ever was on earth, though the fame divine perfon afterwards fuffered much greater indignities *in filence!* For, " Je-
" fus

"*sus answered him,*"——"*If I have spo-*
"*ken evil,*" (said he,) "*bear witness of*
"*the evil: but, if well, why smitest*
"*thou me?*" (V. 23.)

This shews that the reprehension of magistrates and their officers, for *in-justice* and *abuse of power,* is not inconsistent with the strictest rules of *Christian* PASSIVE OBEDIENCE: and, though the apostle Paul, in a similar case, used much harsher language, yet his censure was undoubtedly *just* and *true,* and the severity of his expressions was plainly justified (as I have already shewn) by the event! i. e. *by the fatal catastrophe of* ANANIAS. The law, therefore, which forbids *the speaking evil of the ruler of the people,* is certainly to be understood with proper exceptions, so as not to exclude any just censure of *rulers,* when their *abuse of office,* and the cause of *truth* and *justice,* may render such censure

fure expedient and feafonable. That the apoftle Paul thus underftood the text in queftion, is manifeft from his manner of quoting it, when he was charged with *reviling God's high prieft,* if the feverity of his cenfure be compared with the indifference which he fhewed, immediately afterwards, towards the offended *Sadducee,* by openly profeffing himfelf to be of an oppofite party, and by throwing an oblique charge againft the whole body of Sadducees, as the principal authors of the unjuft perfecution againft himfelf,—" *I am a* Phari-" see," (faid he,) " *the fon of a* Pha-" risee ; *of the hope and refurrection of* " *the dead am I called in queftion."* (Acts xxiii. 6.) Thus he manifeftly threw the whole blame upon *the Sadducees,* and thereby fhewed no inclination to apologize for the feverity of his fpeech to their dignified chief!

I muſt farther remark, that the apoſtle's behaviour, in openly oppoſing the *high prieſt*, (who, as ſuch, was alſo a *chief magiſtrate* and *judge,)* is by no means inconſiſtent with that excellent advice which the ſame apoſtle has laid down in the thirteenth chapter of his Epiſtle to the Romans, though it is frequently cited by the advocates for arbitrary power, in order to juſtify their falſe notions concerning the neceſſity of *abſolute ſubmiſſion and entire paſſive obedience!*

To an inattentive reader, indeed, the apoſtle's expreſſion may ſeem too much to favour ſuch doctrines, if the ſenſe and connexion of the whole context are not carefully weighed together; but though he ſaid,—" *Let every ſoul be*
" *ſubject unto the higher powers. For*
" *there is no power but of God: the pow-*
" *ers that be are ordained of God. Whoſo-*
" *ever*

" ever, therefore, refifteth the power, re-
" fifteth the ordinance of God: and they,
" that refift, fhall receive to themfelves
" damnation." Yet he immediately afterwards fignifies what kind of *rulers* he fpoke of "that were not to be refifted."
" *For* RULERS" (fays he in the very next verfe) " ARE NOT A TERROR TO
" GOOD WORKS, BUT TO THE EVIL.
" *Wilt thou then not be afraid of the*
" *power? do that which is* GOOD, *and thou*
" *fhalt have praife of the fame; for he*
" *is the* MINISTER *of* GOD *to thee for*
" GOOD." (But ANANIAS, as *a ruler*, was certainly the very reverfe of this defcription, fo that the practice of the apoftle, with refpect to him, was by no means oppofite to this doctrine.) " *But*" (fays he) " *if thou do that which is* EVIL,
" *be afraid; for he beareth not the fword*
" *in vain: for he is* THE MINISTER
" OF GOD, *a revenger to* (execute)
" *wrath upon him that doeth evil. Where-*
" *fore* (ye) *muft needs be fubject, not only*
                                            " *for*

"*for wrath, but also* FOR CONSCI-
ENCE SAKE. *For this cause pay ye
tribute also: for they are* GOD'S MINI-
STERS, *attending continually upon
this very thing. Render, therefore, to
all their dues: tribute, to whom tribute* (is due); *custom, to whom custom; fear to whom fear; honour* (12)
to whom honour." (Romans xiii. 1 to 7.) Now, be pleased to remark, that the apostle has expressly and repeatedly assigned the reason why so much respect and obedience is due to the *higher powers*, or to the *ruler*, or *magistrate*; " *for he is*" (says the apostle) *the* MINISTER OF GOD TO THEE FOR GOOD," &c. and again,—"*for he is the* MINISTER OF GOD, *a revenger to wrath upon him that doeth evil:*" and again,—" FOR THEY ARE GOD'S MINISTERS;"— that is, they are *God's ministers* while they

---

(12) See pages 55, 56, and 71, concerning the kind of magistrates to whom honour is or is not *due!*

they maintain *juſtice* and *righteouſneſs* in the execution of their *public* charge, howſoever deficient their characters may be in other reſpects, as *private* individuals; but, on the other hand, ſuch an unjuſt *ruler* as *Ananias*, for inſtance, who *ſat to judge* ACCORDING TO LAW, *and yet commanded a perſon to be beaten* CONTRARY TO LAW, ſuch *a ruler*, I ſay, cannot be eſteemed *a miniſter of God to us* FOR GOOD, or *a miniſter of God* in any reſpect whatſoever. A man, who is notoriouſly guilty of perverting the laws, and of abuſing the delegated power, with which he is entruſted, by acts of *violence* and *injuſtice*, is ſo far from being " *the miniſter of God*," that he is manifeſtly " *the miniſter of the devil*;" which is the expreſs doctrine of *the common law of this kingdom*, according to the moſt approved and moſt antient authorities; wherein we find it applied not merely to inferior *rulers*, but to the ſupreme

preme magistrate, even to the *king* himself, (13) if he *rules* contrary to law,

(13) The celebrated and learned *Henry de Bracton* says,—" *that a king can do nothing else upon earth, as* " *he is* THE MINISTER *and* VICAR OF GOD, *but* " *that only which* BY LAW *he may do*," &c. And, a little farther, he adds,—" *His power, therefore,*" (says he,) " *is of right,* (or law,) *and not of wrong,* (or in- " *jury,*) &c." — " *That a king ought, therefore, to exer-* " *cise the power of right,* (or LAW,) *as* THE VICAR AND " MINISTER OF GOD *on earth, because that power is* " *of* GOD ALONE ; *but the power of* WRONG (OR INJU- " RY) *is of the* DEVIL, *and* NOT OF GOD, *and the* " *work of which so ever of these the king shall do,* " *of him* HE IS THE MINISTER * *whose work he shall do.*
" *While,*

---

* This is perfectly agreeable to the doctrine of holy Scripture ; —" *Whosoever committeth sin*" (said OUR LORD HIMSELF) " *is the* " *servant*" (or minister) " *of sin.*" John viii. 34. Here is no exception or exclusive privilege allowed on account of *temporal dignity,* or *offices* of worldly power ! All men that wilfully *do evil,* (be they *high* or *low,*) are not only *servants of* SIN, but also SONS (as well as servants) OF THE DEVIL, as our Lord himself declared, " *Ye do the deeds of* YOUR FATHER," &c. Ibid. ver. 41. And, when those men, to whom he addressed himself, still contended (notwithstanding their wicked deeds) that they were *the sons and servants of God :* Christ replied, " *Why do ye not understand my speech ?*" &c. — " *Ye are of* (your) *father,* THE DEVIL, *and the lusts of your father* " *ye will do. He was a murderer from the beginning, and abode not in* " *the truth, because there is no truth in him. When he speaketh a lye,* " *he speaketh of his own : for he is a lyar, and the father of it.*" Ibid. ver. 43 and 44. And, in like manner, THE DEVIL is certainly *the* FATHER, or PROMOTER, of every other immorality among men, as
much

law, by violating, corrupting, or perverting, in any respect, the powers of K go-

"*While, therefore, he does* JUSTICE, *he is the* VICAR
" (or MINISTER) *of the* ETERNAL KING; *but he is the*
" MINISTER *of the* DEVIL *while he turns aside to* IN-
" JUSTICE, *for he is called king* (REX) *from* WELL
" RULING, *and not from* REIGNING; *because he is*
" KING *while he* RULES WELL, *but a* TYRANT *while*
" *he oppresses the people committed to his charge with vio-*
" *lent* (or oppressive) *government.*" " Nihil enim aliud
" poteft rex in terris, CUM SIT DEI MINISTER ET
" VICARIUS, nifi id folum quod *de jure* poteft, &c.
" Poteftas itaque fua *juris* eft, et non *injuriæ,* &c.
" Exercere igitur debet rex poteftatem *juris,* ficut
" DEI VICARIUS ET MINISTER *in terra, quia illa*
" *poteftas folius Dei eft,* poteftas autem *injuriæ* DIA-
" BOLI, *non* DEI; et cujus horum opera fecerit rex,
" ejus MINISTER erit, cujus opera fecerit. Igitur *dum*
" *facit juftitiam,* VICARIUS EST REGIS ÆTERNI;
" MINISTER AUTEM DIABOLI, *dum declinet ad inju-*
" *riam.* Dicitur enim rex a bene regendo et non a
" regnando, quia rex eft dum bene regit, tyrannus
" dum populum fibi creditum violenta opprimit
" dominatione." Henrici de Bracton de Legibus et
Confuetudinibus Angliæ lib. iii. c. ix. And nearly
the fame doctrine in fubftance is laid down in Fleta,
lib. i. c. 17.

much as he is of *murder, lying,* and *deceit,* howfoever dignified the
vifible agents therein may be by the inveftiture of temporal honours,
titles, and power, or royal commiffions! — " *Know ye not*" (faid the
apoftle Paul) " *that to whom ye yield yourfelves* SERVANTS *to obey,*
" HIS SERVANTS" (or MINISTERS) " *ye are to whom you obey;*
" *whether of fin unto death, or of obedience unto righteoufnefs!*" Rom.
vi. 6.

government! And that excellent constitutional lawyer, *Lord Sommers*, informs us, that St. Edward's law even goes farther, (14) viz. "*That, unless the king performs his duty, and answers the end for which he was constituted,* not so much AS THE NAME OF A KING *shall remain in him.*" Now, when these constitutional principles of *the English law* are collated and duly compared with the precepts before cited from the apostle Paul, they are so far from being contradictory, that the full and clear meaning of them all may be maintained together without the least inconsistency or discrepance of doctrine; for we may surely say, with the apostle, "*Render to all their dues,*" &c. without seeming to favour the pernicious and dangerous doctrine of an *unlimited passive*

---

(14) The judgement of whole kingdoms and nations, concerning the rights, power, and prerogative, of KINGS, and the rights, privileges, and properties, of the PEOPLE, &c. See the 61st paragraph.

five obedience! " *Render, therefore, to* " *all their dues*; *tribute, to whom tri-* " *bute* (is due); *custom, to whom custom*; " *fear, to whom fear*; *honour, to whom* " *honour.*"—For, though *custom, tribute, fear,* and *honour,* are certainly due to him who is the MINISTER OF GOD *to us for good,* yet, surely, no honour is *due,* or ought to be *rendered,* to THE MINISTER OF THE DEVIL, to the perjured violater of a public trust, who, in the eye of the English law, is not even worthy of " *so much as the name* " *of a king!*"

Fear, indeed, may too often be said to *be due* to such men when in power; but it is a very different sort of *fear* from that reverential *fear* which *is due* to him who " *is the minister of God to* " *us for good!*" It is such *a fear* only as that, which men have of a *wild beast* that devours the flock! He is *fierce* and *strong,*

strong, say they, and, therefore, each individual, through fear of *personal inconvenience to himself,* is induced to wink at the ruinous depredations made upon *his neighbours* and *brethren,* so that, for want of a prudent and timely opposition, the voracious animal (which in a state is a many-headed monster) becomes stronger and more dangerous to the community at large, till the unwary time-servers themselves perceive (when it is too late) that, by their own selfish connivance, respectively, as individuals, they have been accessaries to the general ruin; and, as such, must one day be answerable to God for their shameful breach of that LAW OF LIBERTY, (15) *("* Thou shalt *"* love thy neighbour as thyself,*")* in which we are assured *all the law is fulfilled,* (16) and

(15) See my Tract on the *Law of Liberty.*

(16) " For *all the law is fulfilled* in one word, even " in this; *thou shalt love thy neighbour as thyself.*" Galatians v. 14.

and by which, we are also assured, *we shall be judged!* (17)

This heavenly *principle* is the true and proper ground for *patriotism*, and undoubtedly has always been the predominant motive of great and good men, (such as the disinterested and loyal apostle Paul, following his Lord's example,) in their opposition to the injustice of *rulers* and *magistrates*, though they *passively* submit to personal injuries from other hands! for, in this, as I have already remarked, consists the due distinction between the necessary *Christian submission to personal injuries*, and the doctrine of an *unlimited passive obedience*.

The SUBJECTION and OBEDIENCE to MAGISTRATES, enjoined by the same apostle in his Epistle to Titus, (c. iii. 1.) must certainly be understood with the same

---

(17) " So speak ye, and so do, as they that shall be " JUDGED *by the law of liberty.*" James ii. 12.

fame neceſſary limitations,—" *Put them
" in mind* (ſays the apoſtle) TO BE SUB-
" JECT TO PRINCIPALITIES AND
" POWERS, TO OBEY MAGISTRATES,"
(πειθαρχειν, ſays he, but then he immediately ſubjoins,) "*to be ready to e-
" very good work.*" —— And no man
can be eſteemed "*ready to every good
" work,*" if he is *obedient* to magiſtrates
when their commands exceed the due li-
mits of the law; or if (contrary to the example of the apoſtle himſelf) he neglects a
fair opportunity of publicly diſcounten-
ancing and cenſuring any notorious per-
verſion of *juſtice and right* by a magiſtrate!

The fame neceſſary limitation of the
doctrine of *obedience* muſt alſo be un-
derſtood when we read the exhortation
of another apoſtle on this head, viz.
" *Submit yourſelves to every ordinance
" of man for the Lord's ſake: whether
" it be to the* KING, *as ſupreme;* or
" *unto*

"*unto* GOVERNORS, *as unto them that* "*are sent by him* FOR THE PUNISH-"MENT OF EVIL DOERS, *and for the* "PRAISE OF THEM THAT DO WELL. "*For so is the will of God, that with* "WELL-DOING *ye may put to silence* "*the ignorance of foolish men:* *as free,* "*and not using* (your) *liberty for a cloke* "*of maliciousness, but as the servants of* "*God!*" (1 Peter ii. 13-16.) GOVERNORS are here declared to be sent *for the punishment of evil doers,* and for the *praise of them that do well;* to such, therefore, as answer this description, the *submission* and *honour* enjoined in the context are undoubtedly due; but, whenever the governors themselves become *the evil doers,* and, like *Ananias,* instead of praising and encouraging "*them that do well,*" do notoriously abuse, oppress, and murder, them, *as he did,* (18) it would be a manifest

---

(18) The apostle Paul was so far from retracting any part of his severe censure and remonstrance against Ananias

manifest perversion of the text to suppose that we are required thereby to "*submit ourselves to every ordinance of* "*man*,"

Ananias, that he afterwards (before Felix) defied Ananias and the rest of his accusers to shew that he had been guilty of any the least misdemeanour ever since his last arrival at Jerusalem, and more particularly while "*he stood before the council*," (meaning the time when he foretold that God should smite that *whited wall*, Ananias,) "or else" (said he to Felix) "let these "same here say," (meaning the high priest *Ananias*, the elders, and their orator, Tertullus, mentioned in the first verse of the chapter,) "*if they have found any* "EVIL DOING * IN ME WHILE I STOOD BEFORE THE "COUNCIL, *except it be for this one voice*," (now he once more provokes the malicious Sadducee,) "*that* "*I cried, standing among them, Touching* THE RESUR- "RECTION OF THE DEAD *I am called in question by* "*you this day*." (Acts xxiv. 20.) This is a manifest declaration that there was nothing reprehensible either in his *behaviour* or *words* on that day "before the "*council*," because his declaration concerning the *resurrection of the dead* was the only *one voice* (or expression) which he supposed these Sadducees could call in question and lay to his charge!

* The word in the original is αδικημα, signifying rather *injustice*, or *unrighteousness*, than EVIL-DOING; and as the former may be effected by *words* as well as by *deeds*, this public challenge from the mouth of the apostle includes a complete justification of all that he either *said* or *did* on that day *before the council*.

" *man,*" (19) without admitting such just and necessary exceptions to the doctrine as

(19) The apostles and disciples of Christ were so far "from *submitting themselves to every ordinance of man,*" that they boldly rejected the *unjust* commands even of the high priest and the whole national council of the Jewish state! The great council, called SANHEDRIM, i. e. συνεδριον, (the commands of which they rejected,) included at that time all persons of their nation that bore any public authority or dignity among them, for the text expressly informs us that " *their* RULERS, *and* " ELDERS, *and* SCRIBES, *and* ANNAS, THE HIGH " PRIEST," (and the *high priests* since the time of the Maccabees were generally considered as a sort of princes,) " *and Caiaphas, and John, and Alexander, and as* " *many as were of the kindred of the high priest, were* " *gathered together at Jerusalem.*"

No power, therefore, amongst the Jews, could be more respectable (in regard to temporal authority) than this great national council: and the apostle Peter accordingly acknowledged their legal authority at first, by respectfully addressing them, saying,—" *Ye* " *rulers of the people and elders of Israel,*" &c.

Yet, notwithstanding the temporal authority of this awful assembly of *rulers* and *elders,* (or senators,) they were publicly disregarded and contradicted by the apostles even in their presence, upon the very first proposal of an *unreasonable* and *unlawful* ORDINANCE; for " *they called them,*" (the apostles,) " *and* COMMANDED " THEM *not to speak at all, nor teach in the name of* " *Jesus.*"—But " *Peter and John answered and said* " *unto them, whether it be right in the sight of God to* " *hearken*

as I have already cited from the example of the apostle Paul, and even from that of our Lord himself.

And, therefore, though the apostle Peter adds,—" *Honour all* (men) : *love* " *the brotherhood: fear God: honour* " *the king:*" yet he must necessarily be understood to mean, with the apostle Paul, that we must render " *honour* " *to whom honour*" is DUE, and not to
honour

" *hearken unto you more than unto God, judge ye. For we* " *cannot but speak the things we have seen and heard.*" (Acts iv. 19 and 20.) And afterwards, when they were brought a second time before the said great council to answer for their breach of this " ORDINANCE OF " MAN," " *the high priest asked them, saying,* DID NOT " WE STRAIGHTLY COMMAND YOU *that you should* " *not teach in this name, and behold ye have filled Jeru-* " *salem with your doctrine, and intend to bring this man's* " *blood upon us. Then Peter and the other apostle an-* " *swered and said,*—WE OUGHT TO OBEY GOD RA- " THER THAN MEN," &c. This sentence, in effect, holds good with respect also to the rejection of *every public ordinance* that is contrary to *reason, justice,* or *natural equity,* as well as those that are contrary to *the written word of God!* This I have shewn more at large in my Declaration of the People's Right.

honour such *men* and such *kings* as are unworthy of *honour!* (20)

(20) To the example of the patriotic apostle, Paul, upon this point, I must now add that of another chosen vessel of Christ, the protomartyr *Stephen:* this excellent man, "*full of the Holy Ghost and wisdom,*" (Acts vi. 3.) "*full of faith and power,*" (v. 8.) "*and whose wisdom and spirit none were able to resist:*" (v. 10.)—This excellent man, I say, has left us by his own example an unquestionable precedent on record to demonstrate that HONOUR IS NOT DUE to the highest temporal authority on earth, not even to a *great national council of rulers and elders,* while they exercise their authority in *unjust* prosecutions, and abuse their power by enacting *unreasonable and tyrannical ordinances.* The great council of the Jewish state had "*straightly commanded*" the apostles and disciples of Christ (as I have already remarked in a preceding note) "*not to speak at all, nor teach in the name of Jesus;*" which command, it seems, was given lest their preaching should "*bring this man's blood*" (said the high priest, meaning the blood of our LORD JESUS) "*upon us:*" but *Stephen* paid so little regard either to the *unlawful* command itself, or to the reason of it, that he afterwards publicly upbraided the whole council, with the high priest at the head of it, (in the most stimulating and unreserved terms,) as the betrayers and murderers of that just One!—"*Ye stiff-necked, and un-circumcised in heart and ears,*" (said he to their faces in the public assembly,) "*ye do always resist the Holy Ghost: as your fathers* (did), *so* (do) *ye. Which of the prophets have not your fathers persecuted? And they "have*

But what men (it will be said) are to be esteemed the proper *judges of desert* in such cases, so as to determine with propriety when *honour* is or is not to be rendered? To which I answer, — *Every man* is a judge of it if he be not an idiot or mad man! *Every man* of common sense can distinguish *justice* from *injustice*, *right* from *wrong*, *honourable*

" *have slain them which shewed before of the coming of the*
" JUST ONE, *of whom ye have been now the* BETRAY-
" ERS *and* MURDERERS," &c. (Acts vii. 51 and 52.)
Words could not well be *sharper* than these, which is manifest from their *effect*; for the text testifies that
" *when they heard these things they were* CUT TO THE
" HEART, *and they gnashed on him with* (their) *teeth*."
(V. 54.) Thus it clearly appears that the holy, innocent, and meek Stephen did not think himself bound (like our undistinguishing *passive-obedience* men) to " *sub-
" mit to every ordinance of man,*" &c. nor to " *honour all
" men*," without making reasonable and due exceptions! Nay, so far from *honouring* men merely on account of their *temporal dignity*, it is manifest that he treated the whole *body of rulers* with the utmost severity and contempt, while he thought them *unworthy of honour*, and yet there is no doubt but that he most conscientiously, on every occasion, rendered " *honour to whom
" honour*" WAS DUE!

honourable from *dishonourable*, (21) whenever he happens to be an eye or ear witness of the proper circumstances of evidence for such a judgement! *Every man*, (except as above,) be he ever so poor and mean with respect to his rank in this life, inherits *the knowledge of good and evil*, or REASON, from the common parents of mankind, and is thereby rendered answerable to GOD for *all* his actions, and answerable to MAN for *many* of them!

In this *hereditary knowledge*, and in the proper use of it, (according to the different stations of life in which men subsist in this world,) consists the *equality* of ALL MANKIND in the sight of GOD, and also in the eye of *the law*, I mean the *common law* and rules of *natural justice*, which are formed upon the self-evident

(21) See my Tract on " *the Law of Nature and the* " *Principles of Action in Man*," wherein, I hope, this point is fully demonstrated.

evident conclusions of *human reason*, and are the necessary result of the above-mentioned *hereditary knowledge in* MAN. Every man *knows*, by what we call *conscience*, (which is only an effect of *human reason* upon the mind,) whether his own actions deserve the *censure* of the *magistrate*, who " bears not the " *sword in vain!*" And the same principle of *hereditary knowledge* enables him to judge also concerning the outward actions of *other men*, whether they be *just* or *unjust*; whether they be *praiseworthy* or *censurable!*

But, if a man abuses his own *natural reason*, and suffers himself to be blinded by private interest, by passion, or unreasonable resentment, or by pride, envy, or personal partiality, and is thereby led to misconstrue the actions of his superiors, to behave unseemly towards them, and to censure them publicly

licly without a juſt cauſe, the *conſcience* of ſuch an offender againſt *reaſon* will ſpeedily inform him that he has cauſe to *fear the magiſtrate,* and that he is liable to ſuffer for his miſbehaviour " *as an evil doer:*" but, when the like faults are diſcoverable on the other ſide, that is, on the ſide of the ſuperior or magiſtrate, (as it happened in the caſe of Ananias,) a *juſt* cenſure of the *unjuſt* magiſtrate, even though it comes from the pooreſt and meaneſt man that happens to be preſent, will have its due weight in the opinion of all unprejudiced and diſintereſted perſons, and may occaſion a conſiderable check to the progreſs of *injuſtice;* and, therefore, if any man neglects ſuch an opportunity (when he has it in his power) of making a perſonal *proteſt* (as Paul did) againſt the public injuſtice of a wicked magiſtrate, he ſtrengthens the hand of iniquity by his timidity and

and remissness, and becomes accessary to the public disgrace by refusing his endeavours, according to his abilities, (howsoever small,) to vindicate the *laws of God*, and maintain the *common rights of his neighbours and brethren.* Such an one unhappily demonstrates that he has more *fear* of MAN than of GOD, and much more *love* for *himself* than he has for his *neighbour* and *country*, and, consequently, in that awful day, when he " *shall be judged by the law of liber-* " *ty,*" (22) must be liable, (unless a timely repentance should have previously restored him to a better use of that *hereditary knowledge* for which all men are accountable,) must be liable, I say, " to be cast with *the unprofitable ser-* " *vant into outer darkness: there shall* " *be weeping and gnashing of teeth!*" Matth. xxv. 30.

ALL

---

(22) James ii. 12. See also my Tract on *the Law of Liberty.*

ALL MEN, therefore, be they ever so *rich*, or ever so *poor* and *mean*, are REQUIRED to vindicate the cause of *truth, justice,* and *righteousness*, whenever they have a favourable opportunity of doing so; they ARE REQUIRED, I say, because they ARE ENABLED by their NATURAL KNOWLEDGE of GOOD and EVIL to discern and judge concerning the *fitness* or *unfitness* of human actions, and of the *justice* or *injustice* of all measures and proceedings that happen to fall within the reach of their inspection and consequent observation. He, who denies this, is ignorant of the *true dignity of human nature*, and wants a teacher to point out to him not only *the equality of mankind before God*, but also *the universal conditions of man's subsistence in the world!*——THE HEREDITARY KNOWLEDGE OF GOOD AND EVIL may, at least, be esteemed as the ONE TALENT

for

for which *all mankind* are accountable to the universal Lord! And, therefore, if they wilfully *abuse* or *bury* THIS TALENT, they have surely nothing to expect but the condemnation abovementioned of the *unprofitable servant!*

Shall we blame the patriotic apostle, then, for his zeal in vindicating *the natural rights of mankind* against an UNJUST JUDGE, when he had so fair an opportunity of protesting against his iniquity? God forbid! Let us, on the contrary, revere his example, which, in reality, affords no opposition to the doctrine laid down in the beginning of this Tract concerning the necessity of "*Christian submission to personal injuries.*" If he, sometimes, freely and courageously expressed his *resentment for personal ill usage,* (23) it was always

---

(23) In pursuing the examination of this subject concerning *resentment for personal ill usage,* I was gradually led

ways in vindication of *the law*, on which (next to the providence of God) the safety, liberty, and happiness, of the community depend; whereas, the *hasty revenger of his own cause* is so far from being a friend to the community, or a *lover of liberty*, that he himself is actually *a tyrant*; because he neglects the necessary doctrine of "*Chris-*" *tian submission to personal injuries,*" and on every occasion is ready to revenge his *own cause* with his *own hand*, and to usurp all the distinct offices of judge,

---

led to consider the present unnatural though prevailing practice of DUELLING; and this occasioned my "*Re-*" *marks on the Opinions of some of the most eminent Wri-*" *ters on* CROWN LAW, *respecting the due distinction* " *between* MANSLAUGHTER *and* MURDER," (printed in 1773,) which Remarks were, at first, intended as a continuation of this tract; but finding, soon afterwards, that some publication, to correct the common mistaken doctrines concerning *manslaughter* and *duelling*, was become more immediately necessary, I thought it adviseable to detach what I had written on that subject from this tract, and to print it as soon as possible, (with some few alterations and additions,) rather than to wait for the publication of these other tracts.

judge, jury, and executioner! He is fo far from vindicating *the law*, like the generous and patriotic apoftle, for the fake of *national liberty*, that he manifeftly fets himfelf up *above the law*, (which is *the firft characteriftic of a tyrant,*) and thereby renders himfelf in fact an open enemy to *liberty*, and confequently *a difgrace to fociety!*

GRANVILLE SHARP.

" GLORY to GOD in the Higheft!
" And on Earth — PEACE,
" GOOD WILL towards Men!"

INDEX

INDEX

OF

Texts referred to in the foregoing Work.

Leviticus.

Chap.	Verses.	Pages.
xxv.	52.	18.

Deuteronomy.

xv.	12, 14.	21.

Ecclesiasticus.

xxxiii.	12.	34 n.

Isaiah.

liii.	7, 8.	64 n.

Matthew.

v.	17.	63 n.
xxiii.	24, 25.	61.
	27, 28. }	61.
	30, 33. }	
xxv.	30.	88.

Mark.

ix.	6.	58 n.

Luke.

Chap.	Verses.	Pages.
vi.	28, 29.	39.
xiii.	32.	62.

John.

viii.	34.	72 n.
	41.	72 n.
	43, 44.	72 n.
xv.	12 to 15.	37 n.
xviii.	21, 22.	65.
	23.	66.
	36.	7.

Acts.

iv.	8.	83 n.
	10.	83 n.
	19, 20.	83 n.
vii.	51, 52.	84 n.
	54.	84 n.
xvi.	30 to 39.	44 n.
xxii.	24 to 30.	45 n.
xxiii.	1 to 5.	45 n.

Acts continued.

xxiii.	6.	67.
xxiv.	20.	80 n.

Romans.

ii.	11.	34 n.
vi.	6.	73 n.
xiii.		68.
	1 to 7	70.
	9, 10.	37 n.

1 Corinthians.

vi.	19, 20.	23.
vii.	21.	7.
	20, 21.	16.
	21 to 23.	12 n.
	21.	17.
	22.	17.
	23.	17. 20.

Galatians.

v.	14.	76 n.

Ephesians.

vi.	5 to 8.	7. 15.
	5, &c.	34.
	8, 9.	34 n.

Colossians.

iii.	2.	15.

Colossians continued.

iii.	18.	32 n.
	20.	33 n.
	22.	33 n.
	22, 23.	7.
	23, 24.	33 n.
	24.	34 n.
	25.	31 n. 34 n.
iv.	1.	35 n. 36 n.

1 Timothy.

vi.		32 n.
	1 to 8.	11.
	1.	14. 38.
	2.	24. 28.

Titus.

ii.	9.	32 n.
	9, 10.	11.
	10.	14. 32.
iii.	1.	77.

James.

ii.	12.	77 n. 84 n.

1 Peter.

ii.	13 to 16.	79.
	18.	15.

INDEX

INDEX

OF THE

Different Authors referred to.

A.

ASSEMBLY's ANNOTATIONS, 57 n.
Ananias, 49 n.
Ananus, 49 n.
Auguſtine, biſhop of Hippo, 57 n.

B.

Benſon, (Dr. Geo.) 25 n.
Borner, 26 n.
Bracton, (Hen. de,) 72 n. 73 n.
Broughton, (Hugh,) 47 n.

C.

Caſtalio, 47 n.
Cornelius a Lapide, 58.

F.

Fleta, 73 n.
Fox, (reverend Francis,) 59 n.
Francowitz, (Mat. Flac.) 57 n. 58 n.

G.
Grotius, 59 n.

H.
Hammond, 28.
Heinsius, 47 n.

J.
Josephus, 52 n. 53 n. 57 n.
Judgement of whole kingdoms and nations, &c. 74 n.
Justin Martyr, 21.

K.
Kuster, 26 n.

L.
Law of Liberty, 76 n. 86 n.
Law of Nature, 85 n.
Lightfoot, 59 n.
Lorinus, 57.

M.
Martin, (monf.) 58 n.
Mill, (Dr.) 26 n.

P.
Pet. 2 and 3. MSS. so called, 26 n.

S.
Sommers, (lord,) 73.
Syriac version, 25 n.

T.
Tertullian, 21.

W.
Whiston, 54 n.
Whitby, (Dr.) 59 n. 21. 25 n. 34 n.

INDEX

INDEX

OF THE

Various Topics discussed in this Work.

A.

Ananias. See FRANCOWITZ, MARTIN, also *high priest*, *judge*, and *magistrate*. St. Paul's denunciation against him justified by the event, 52 n. his injustice and cruelty towards the Christians, 53 n.

Apostles. Did not submit themselves to every ordinance of man without exception, 78 & seq.

Author. A learned and reverend correspondent differs from him in his notions of slavery, 4; his character of that correspondent, 5; concessions of his, 6, 13; reasons for not answering a letter from him at the time of receiving it, ib. his design in this treatise is to demonstrate the absolute illegality of slavery among Christians, 7; esteems both master and slaves as brethren, 12; his reasons for printing his Remarks on the Crown Law prior to this tract, 91 n.

B.

Believers. God alone their judge, 26.

C.

Christ. His disciples had no commission to alter the temporary conditions of men, 7; claimed no authority to dispense with the Mosaic law, 62 n.

Conscience. Only an effect of human reason, 86.

Correspondent of the Author's. See *Author.* Does not think Christianity released slaves, &c. 6; an opinion of his examined, 18 n. & seq. another, 30 n. & seq.

D.

Duties of placability, submission, and patience, too commonly misunderstood or rejected by the Christian world, 41.

E.

Edward, (St.). The strictness of his law concerning kings, 74 & seq.

Egyptian bondage. A type of our spiritual servitude to the enemy of mankind, 20.

F.

Fear. That we have of a tyrant very different from that we have of a good magistrate, 75.

Francowitz, (Mat. Flac.). His opinion of St. Paul's answer to Ananias, 57 n.

Freedom. The attainment of it legally enjoined servants by St. Paul, 12 n. 16.

G.

GOD. Submission in servants enjoined for conscience sake towards him, 15 & seq. masters and servants equal in his sight, 17. See *Believers, Judge.*

Good and evil. See *Reason.*

Good

Good men. From whence their zeal arises for just and equitable laws, 42.

Grotius. Quoted by Dr. Whitby concerning St. Paul's reply to Ananias, 59 n.

H.

High priest. St. Paul's spirited but cautious behaviour before him, 46 & seq. did not attempt to excuse or apologize for it, 47 & seq. 67 ; the justness of that behaviour, 56. 60. 90 ; Lorinus' paraphrase of the apostle's reply to him, 57 ; which is strictly consonant to reason and natural right, 59 ; our Lord's behaviour, in the same predicament, exactly similar, 60 & seq. the apostle's behaviour not inconsistent with his doctrine, Rom. xiii. 68 & seq. which behaviour he afterwards defended before Felix, 79 n.

J.

Jews. Not to be sold as bondmen, 18, 19, 20. See *Slavery*.

Injustice. Censuring bad magistrates may tend to check its progress, 87 ; which is the duty of every man, 89.

Interrogatories. Their illegality, 64.

Judge. One who perverts judgement degrades himself from his office, 55 ; our Saviour's character of such, 61 & seq. who cannot be deemed ministers of God in any respect, 71.

K.

Kings. Are not *ministers of God* when they act contrary to law, 72 ; and see the notes on that and the succeeding page. See *Edward* (St.) ; not worthy the name of a king, 75 ; but are *ministers of the devil*, and unworthy of *honour* while they do evil, ib.

L.

Law. A notorious breach of it by a ruler is a temporary disqualification, 55. See *Kings, Edward* (St.).
Loyal. What it is to be really so, 56.

M.

Magistrates. Their reprehension not inconsistent with Christian passive obedience, 66 & seq. good one. See *Fear, Injustice.*
Martin, (mons.). Agrees with M. Flac. Francowitz, Grotius, Whitby, &c. concerning St. Paul's reply to Ananias, 58 n.
Masters. See GOD, *Slavery.*
Ministers of God. See *Kings.*
Ministers of the devil. See *Kings.*

O.

Obedience. See *Servants.*
Oppression. That practised by the slave-holders no more justified by the New Testament than that of strikers or robbers, 41.

P.

Passive obedience. See *Magistrates.* Not due to evil magistrates, 77 & seq.
Patience. See *Duties.*
Patriotism. The proper ground for it, 77.
Paul, (St.). His zeal for the Roman liberty, 42; his Christian patience and meekness under personal injuries, 43. 44 n. See *high priest.* His injunction, Tit. iii. 1. explained, 77.
Peter, (St.). His injunction, 1 Pet. ii. 13 to 16. explained, 79.
Price. The meaning of that word in 1 Cor. vii. 23. examined, 21 & seq.

Q.

Q.

Questions. Serious ones to the slave-holders, 30 & seq.

R.

Reason. Inherited by all men, except idiots or mad men, 84. 89; which renders all men equal in the sight of God and the law, 85. See *Conscience*. The talent for which all men are accountable, 90.

Royal law. No single text to be depended on, which will not bear the test of it, 27.

Ruler. See *Law*.

S.

Sanhedrim. Its power and dignity, 81 n.

Scriptures. Their honour what the author has most at heart, 4.

Servants, (Christian,). Their obedience frequently insisted on by St. Paul, 8 & seq. the submission required of them does not imply the legality of slave-holding, 11; on what principles that submission is founded, 13 & seq. 24 n. which do not admit of any right or property in the master, 15; submission enjoined by St. Peter both to the good and bad master, for conscience' sake towards God, 15 & seq. See GOD, *Slavery, Slave-holders, Tyranny*.

Slave-holders. Cannot avail themselves of any of the texts relating to Christian servants, 29. 38. See *Questions, Oppression*.

Slavery. Some particular texts seem to prove the toleration of it amongst the primitive Christians, 3. See *Author*. No more than a state of hired servitude among the Jews, 19 n. 21 n. the text 1 Tim. vi. 2. no argument in favour of it, 24 & seq. that text intended for servants, not masters, 26; so understood by by Dr. Hammond, 26; the texts which juſtify the ſlave's ſubmiſſion do not authorize the maſter's tyranny, 10. (See the whole note in that page.) 40.

Subjection (unlimited). Inconſiſtent with the dignity of a Chriſtian, 17; and intirely illegal, ib. See *Duties*.

T.

Texts. See *Price*, *Slavery*, *Whitby*, *Paul*, *Peter*.

Tyrants See *Fear*. The folly and wickedneſs of abetting them, 76; characteriſtics of one, 91.

Tyranny. The ſubmiſſion enjoined in the goſpel no plea for it, 39.

W.

Whitby, (Dr.). Miſtakes the meaning of the text 1 Cor. vii. 23, 21; is of the ſame opinion with Grotius concerning St. Paul's reply to Ananias, 59 n.

Whited wall. The propriety of that expreſſion of St. Paul, 52.

THE END.

www.ingramcontent.com/pod-product-compliance
Lightning Source LLC
Chambersburg PA
CBHW030436190426
43202CB00036B/1569